Android Fragments

Dave MacLean
Satya Komatineni

Apress®

Android Fragments

ISBN-13 (pbk): 978-1-4842-0854-0

ISBN-13 (electronic): 978-1-4842-0853-3

Managing Director: Welmoed Spahr
Lead Editor: Steve Anglin
Technical Reviewer: Shane Kirk
Editorial Board: Steve Anglin, Ewan Buckingham, Gary Cornell, Louise Corrigan, James T. DeWolf, Jonathan Gennick, Jonathan Hassell, Robert Hutchinson, Michelle Lowman, James Markham, Matthew Moodie, Jeff Olson, Jeffrey Pepper, Douglas Pundick, Ben Renow-Clarke, Dominic Shakeshaft, Gwenan Spearing, Matt Wade, Steve Weiss
Coordinating Editor: Mark Powers
Copy Editor: Brendan Frost
Compositor: SPi Global
Indexer: SPi Global
Artist: SPi Global
Cover Designer: Anna Ishchenko

Distributed to the book trade worldwide by Springer Science+Business Media New York, 233 Spring Street, 6th Floor, New York, NY 10013. Phone 1-800-SPRINGER, fax (201) 348-4505, e-mail orders-ny@springer-sbm.com, or visit www.springeronline.com. Apress Media, LLC is a California LLC and the sole member (owner) is Springer Science + Business Media Finance Inc (SSBM Finance Inc). SSBM Finance Inc is a Delaware corporation.

For information on translations, please e-mail rights@apress.com, or visit www.apress.com.

Apress and friends of ED books may be purchased in bulk for academic, corporate, or promotional use. eBook versions and licenses are also available for most titles. For more information, reference our Special Bulk Sales–eBook Licensing web page at www.apress.com/bulk-sales.

Any source code or other supplementary material referenced by the author in this text is available to readers at www.apress.com/9781484208540. For detailed information about how to locate your book's source code, go to www.apress.com/source-code/.

To my dog Artoo who, like this book, is a wonderful little new addition to the family.

—Dave

To my 10-year-old son Narayan Komatineni, who teaches me to think fearlessly on a daily basis.

—Satya

Contents at a Glance

Contents

About the Authors

Dave MacLean is a software engineer and architect living and working in Orlando, Florida. Since 1980, he has programmed in many languages, developing solutions ranging from robot automation systems to data warehousing, from web self-service applications to electronic data interchange transaction processors. Dave has worked for Sun Microsystems, IBM, Trimble Navigation, General Motors, Blue Cross Blue Shield of Florida and several small companies. He has written several books on Android and a few magazine articles. He graduated from the University of Waterloo in Canada with a degree in systems design engineering. Visit his blog at http://davemac327.blogspot.com or contact him at davemac327@gmail.com.

Satya Komatineni has been programming for more than 20 years in the IT and Web space. He has had the opportunity to work with Assembly, C, C++, Rexx, Java, C#, Lisp, HTML, JavaScript, CSS, SVG, relational databases, object databases and related technologies. He has published more than 30 articles touching many of these areas, both in print and online. He has been a frequent speaker at O'Reilly Open Source Conference, speaking on innovations around Java and Web. Satya has done a considerable amount of original work in creating Aspire, a comprehensive open-source Java-based web framework, and has explored personal web productivity and collaboration tools through his open-source work for KnowledgeFolders.com. Satya holds a master's degree in electrical engineering from Indian Institute of Technology and a bachelor's degree in electrical engineering from Andhra University, India. You can find his website at SatyaKomatineni.com.

About the Technical Reviewer

Shane Kirk earned a B.S. in Computer Science from the University of Kentucky in 2000. He's currently a Senior Software Engineer for IDEXX Laboratories in Westbrook, Maine, where he spends his days working on communication solutions for embedded systems. Shane's foray into mobile development began in 2010, shortly after purchasing his first smartphone - a Droid X running Eclair (Android 2.1). He's been hooked on Android ever since.

Acknowledgments

Writing a technical book is a team effort, and we'd like to thank this team in particular. The folks at Apress were great, including Steve Anglin, Mark Powers, Brendan Frost and Anna Ishchenko. We'd also like to graciously thank our technical reviewer Shane Kirk, who worked hard to catch our slips and who made this book so much better.

We have also been ably assisted by the various Android forums that have provided answers to our questions as well as valuable advice. We extend our thanks to our readers. We greatly appreciate your picking up our books, asking us questions, and keeping us on our toes. We are better for it, and we hope our work can somehow help you achieve your goals. We work very hard to stay abreast of all things Android, in a way that allows us to explain it to you so it's easy to understand. We really hope you will learn a lot from it, as we did.

We especially want to thank our families, for letting us go off to do research, buy gadgets, vent our frustrations, and ultimately create this work you now hold. We are forever indebted to you.

Introduction

Mobile application development is as hot a topic as ever. Consumers have been benefiting from smartphones for years, and now more and more companies are getting into the game. Some developers are learning mobile development brand new, while others are coming from backgrounds in web development or PC programming. No matter, making mobile applications that work well requires learning some new concepts and skills. With Android in particular, fragments are one of those topics that are critical to an Android application, but are not that easy to master. Once you understand the inner details of how fragments work, and the ways in which they can be used, you will find it much easier to design and build Android applications.

Fragments are conceptual containers of user interface and logic that can be easily combined as building blocks into your mobile application. Android has not abandoned the `Activity` class, but activities are now often composed from fragments. This makes it much easier to build applications to support different device types, sizes and orientations.

This book, *Android Fragments*, is our sixth book on Android. In the first four books, published under the *Pro Android* name, we covered many of the Android APIs, from basic Views to broadcast receivers, touchscreens, services and animations. In *Expert Android* we tackled more advanced Android APIs as well as the advanced debugging capabilities of Android.

Android Fragments is actually a subset of the *Pro Android* book. It focuses specifically on fragments, providing you with the detail you won't find in other books. It covers not only the basic fragment, but also dialog fragments, preference fragments, and progress dialog fragments. It covers the compatibility library so you can use fragments with the older versions of Android that originally did not support fragments. After reading this book, you should have no fear incorporating all manner of fragments into your applications.

Is This Book for You?

This book was written for the mobile developer who has a good understanding of Android, and the basics of an Android application, but who needs or wants an in-depth understanding of fragments. A good architect knows the materials. To build great mobile applications, the great mobile developer needs to know fragments. If you don't know, or if you're not sure you understand fragments well, then this book is for you.

What You Need to Know Before You Begin

Android Fragments assumes that you are familiar with Java and basic Android and that you have developed Android applications, using Eclipse or another IDE. You do not need to be an Android expert.

With that said, here's a brief, quick overview of what is in *Android Fragments*, chapter by chapter.

What's in This Book

We start *Android Fragments* by documenting in depth the Fragment class and its life cycle. We cover the careful integration dance between the activities and the fragments of an application. You'll see how to incorporate fragments into the UI, but also how to encapsulate functionality into fragments.

Chapter 2 helps you understand what happens to a fragment during a configuration change, such as the rotation of a device. You'll see how fragments make this easier than it has been in the past.

Dialogs are very common in applications, and now you'll be using fragments to display them. Find out how in Chapter 3.

Preferences also went through some major UI changes when fragments came along. Chapter 4 covers everything you need to know about using Android's preference framework for preferences or for just a quick and easy way to store some application state from one invocation to the next.

Android fragmentation has to do with the many different versions of Android that exist in the world at the same time. And while it is not about fragments, you'll want to know how to use fragments on older versions of Android that pre-date the introduction of fragments. Google has made it possible through the use of compatibility libraries, so Chapter 5 shows you how to use them. After reading this chapter you'll be able to write one application, with fragments, and have it supported on devices as old as Froyo (Android 2.2).

This mini book wraps up with a chapter on AsyncTask, an extremely useful construct for doing work in the background of an application, while at the same time being able to update a UI that's rendered in, you guessed it, fragments.

All throughout the book, numerous sample programs are explained with code listings. The complete sample programs are all downloadable from our website, so you'll be able to easily follow along, and have a great starter set of working applications for experimentation and for starting your own applications.

How to Prepare for Android Fragments

Although we have used the latest Android release (5.0) to write and test *Android Fragments*, the contents of this book are fairly independent of any Android release. Most, if not all, sample programs and code should work even in future releases. To heighten the readability of these chapters, among other improvements we have reduced the typical pages and pages of source code. Instead, the source code for each chapter is available both on apress.com and at our supporting site, androidbook.com. We still include source code in the text, but it will be the important code that you want to see to understand the concepts.

You will be able to download each chapter's source code and load it into Eclipse directly. If you are using IntelliJ or another editor, you can unzip each chapter and build the code by importing the projects manually into your favorite IDE.

If you are programming using any of the topics that we have covered in any of our books, including *Android Fragments,* remember that our websites androidbook.com and satyakomatineni.com have dedicated knowledge folders for each topic. These knowledge folders document various items in each topic. For example, you will see in this book the Android API links you will need as you develop code in that context. In short, we use these sites often to grab code snippets and also quickly get to the Android API links.

How to Reach Us

We can be reached readily via our respective e-mail addresses: Dave MacLean at davemac327@gmail.com and Satya Komatineni at satya.komatineni@gmail.com. Also, keep this URL in your bookmarks: http://www.androidbook.com. Here you will find links to source code, links to downloadable projects, key feedback from readers, full contact information, future notifications, errata, news on our future projects, a reading guide, and additional resources.

We truly hope that you enjoy our book, and we welcome your feedback.

Chapter 1

Fragments Fundamentals

For the first two major releases of Android, small screens were it. Then came the Android tablets: devices with screen sizes of 10". And that complicated things. Why? Because now there was so much screen real estate that a simple activity had a hard time filling a screen while at the same time keeping to a single function. It no longer made sense to have an e-mail application that showed only headers in one activity (filling a large screen), and a separate activity to show an individual e-mail (also filling a large screen). With that much room to work with, an application could show a list of e-mail headers down the left side of the screen and the selected e-mail contents on the right side of the screen. Could it be done in a single activity with a single layout? Well, yes, but you couldn't reuse that activity or layout for any of the smaller-screen devices.

One of the core classes introduced in Android 3.0 was the Fragment class, especially designed to help developers manage application functionality so it would provide great usability as well as lots of reuse. This chapter will introduce you to the fragment, what it is, how it fits into an application's architecture, and how to use it. Fragments make a lot of interesting things possible that were difficult before. At about the same time, Google released a fragment SDK that works on old Androids. So even if you weren't interested in writing applications for tablets, you may have found that fragments made your life easier on non-tablet devices. Now it's easier than ever to write great applications for smartphones and tablets and even TVs and other devices.

Let's get started with Android fragments.

What Is a Fragment?

This first section will explain what a fragment is and what it does. But first, let's set the stage to see why we need fragments. As you learned earlier, an Android application on small-screen devices uses activities to show data and functionality to a user, and each activity has a fairly simple, well-defined purpose. For example, an activity might show the user a list of contacts from their address book. Another activity might allow the user to type an e-mail. The Android application is the series of these activities grouped together to achieve a larger purpose, such as managing an e-mail account via the reading and sending of messages. This is fine for a small-screen device, but when the user's screen is very large (10" or larger), there's room on the screen to do more than just one simple thing. An application might want to let the user view the list of e-mails in their inbox and at the same time show the currently selected e-mail text next to the list. Or an application might want to show a list of contacts and at the same time show the currently selected contact in a detail view.

As an Android developer, you know that this functionality could be accomplished by defining yet another layout for the xlarge screen with ListViews and layouts and all sorts of other views. And by "yet another layout" we mean layouts in addition to those you've probably already defined for the smaller screens. Of course, you'll want to have separate layouts for the portrait case as well as the landscape case. And with the size of an xlarge screen, this could mean quite a few views for all the labels and fields and images and so on that you'll need to lay out and then provide code for. If only there were a way to group these view objects together and consolidate the logic for them, so that chunks of an application could be reused across screen sizes and devices, minimizing how much work a developer has to do to maintain their application. And that is why we have fragments.

One way to think of a fragment is as a sub-activity. And in fact, the semantics of a fragment are a lot like an activity. A fragment can have a view hierarchy associated with it, and it has a life cycle much like an activity's life cycle. Fragments can even respond to the Back button like activities do. If you were thinking, "If only I could put multiple activities together on a tablet's screen at the same time," then you're on the right track. But because it would be too messy to have more than one activity of an application active at the same time on a tablet screen, fragments were created to implement basically that thought. This means fragments are contained within an activity. Fragments can only exist within the context of an activity; you can't use a fragment without an activity. Fragments can coexist with other elements of an activity, which means you do *not* need to convert the entire user interface of your activity to use fragments. You can create an activity's layout as before and only use a fragment for one piece of the user interface.

Fragments are not like activities, however, when it comes to saving state and restoring it later. The fragments framework provides several features to make saving and restoring fragments much slmpler than the work you need to do on activities.

How you decide when to use a fragment depends on a few considerations, which are discussed next.

When to Use Fragments

One of the primary reasons to use a fragment is so you can reuse a chunk of user interface and functionality across devices and screen sizes. This is especially true with tablets. Think of how much can happen when the screen is as large as a tablet's. It's more like a desktop than a phone, and many of your desktop applications have a multipane user interface. As described earlier, you can have a list and a detail view of the selected item on screen at the same time. This is easy to picture in a landscape orientation with the list on the left and the details on the right. But what if the user rotates the device to portrait mode so that now the screen is taller than it is wide? Perhaps you now want the list to be in the top portion of the screen and the details in the bottom portion. But what if this application is running on a small screen and there's just no room for the two portions to be on the screen at the same time? Wouldn't you want the separate activities for the list and for the details to be able to share the logic you've built into these portions for a large screen? We hope you answered yes. Fragments can help with that. Figure 1-1 makes this a little clearer.

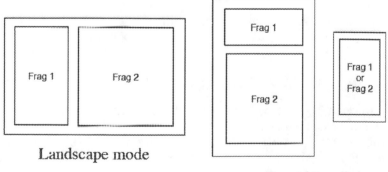

Figure 1-1. *Fragments used for a tablet UI and for a smartphone UI*

In landscape mode, two fragments may sit nicely side by side. In portrait mode, we might be able to put one fragment above the other. But if we're trying to run the same application on a device with a smaller screen, we might need to show either fragment 1 or fragment 2 but not both at the same time. If we tried to manage all these scenarios with layouts, we'd be creating quite a few, which means difficulty trying to keep everything correct across many separate layouts. When using fragments, our layouts stay simple; each activity layout deals with the fragments as containers, and the activity layouts don't need to specify the internal structure of each fragment. Each fragment will have its own layout for its internal structure and can be reused across many configurations.

Let's go back to the rotating orientation example. If you've had to code for orientation changes of an activity, you know that it can be a real pain to save the current state of the activity and to restore the state once the activity has been re-created. Wouldn't it be nice if your activity had chunks that could be easily retained across orientation changes, so you could avoid all the tearing down and re-creating every time the orientation changed? Of course it would. Fragments can help with that.

Now imagine that a user is in your activity, and they've been doing some work. And imagine that the user interface has changed within the same activity, and the user wants to go back a step, or two, or three. In an old-style activity, pressing the Back button will take the user out of the activity entirely. With fragments, the Back button can step backward through a stack of fragments while staying inside the current activity.

Next, think about an activity's user interface when a big chunk of content changes; you'd like to make the transition look smooth, like a polished application. Fragments can do that, too.

Now that you have some idea of what a fragment is and why you'd want to use one, let's dig a little deeper into the structure of a fragment.

The Structure of a Fragment

As mentioned, a fragment is like a sub-activity: it has a fairly specific purpose and almost always displays a user interface. But where an activity is subclassed from `Context`, a fragment is extended from `Object` in package `android.app`. A fragment is *not* an extension of `Activity`. Like activities, however, you will always extend `Fragment` (or one of its subclasses) so you can override its behavior.

A fragment can have a view hierarchy to engage with a user. This view hierarchy is like any other view hierarchy in that it can be created (inflated) from an XML layout specification or created in code. The view hierarchy needs to be attached to the view hierarchy of the surrounding activity if it is to be seen by the user, which you'll get to shortly. The view objects that make up a fragment's view hierarchy are the same sorts of views that are used elsewhere in Android. So everything you know about views applies to fragments as well.

Besides the view hierarchy, a fragment has a bundle that serves as its initialization arguments. Similar to an activity, a fragment can be saved and later restored automatically by the system. When the system restores a fragment, it calls the default constructor (with no arguments) and then restores this bundle of arguments to the newly created fragment. Subsequent callbacks on the fragment have access to these arguments and can use them to get the fragment back to its previous state. For this reason, it is imperative that you

- Ensure that there's a default constructor for your fragment class.

- Add a bundle of arguments as soon as you create a new fragment so these subsequent methods can properly set up your fragment, and so the system can restore your fragment properly when necessary.

An activity can have multiple fragments in play at one time; and if a fragment has been switched out with another fragment, the fragment-switching transaction can be saved on a back stack. The back stack is managed by the fragment manager tied to the activity. The back stack is how the Back button behavior is managed. The fragment manager is discussed later in this chapter. What you need to know here is that a fragment knows which activity it is tied to, and from there it can get to its fragment manager. A fragment can also get to the activity's resources through its activity.

Also similar to an activity, a fragment can save state into a bundle object when the fragment is being re-created, and this bundle object gets given back to the fragment's onCreate() callback. This saved bundle is also passed to onInflate(), onCreateView(), and onActivityCreated(). Note that this is not the same bundle as the one attached as initialization arguments. This bundle is one in which you are likely to store the current state of the fragment, not the values that should be used to initialize it.

A Fragment's Life Cycle

Before you start using fragments in sample applications, you need understand the life cycle of a fragment. Why? A fragment's life cycle is more complicated than an activity's life cycle, and it's very important to understand *when* you can do things with fragments. Figure 1-2 shows the life cycle of a fragment.

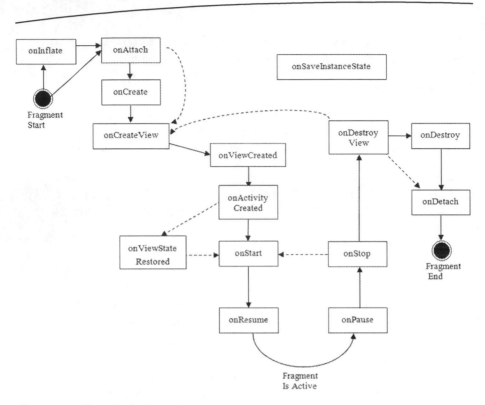

Figure 1-2. Life cycle of a fragment

If you compare this to the life cycle for an activity, you'll notice several differences, due mostly to the interaction required between an activity and a fragment. A fragment is very dependent on the activity in which it lives and can go through multiple steps while its activity goes through one.

At the very beginning, a fragment is instantiated. It now exists as an object in memory. The first thing that is likely to happen is that initialization arguments will be added to your fragment object. This is definitely true in the situation where the system is re-creating your fragment from a saved state. When the system is restoring a fragment from a saved state, the default constructor is invoked, followed by the attachment of the initialization arguments bundle. If you are doing the creation of the fragment in code, a nice pattern to use is that in Listing 1-1, which shows a factory type of instantiator within the MyFragment class definition.

Listing 1-1. Instantiating a Fragment Using a Static Factory Method

```
public static MyFragment newInstance(int index) {
    MyFragment f = new MyFragment();
    Bundle args = new Bundle();
    args.putInt("index", index);
    f.setArguments(args);
    return f;
}
```

From the client's point of view, they get a new instance by calling the static newInstance() method with a single argument. They get the instantiated object back, and the initialization argument has been set on this fragment in the arguments bundle. If this fragment is saved and reconstructed later, the system will go through a very similar process of calling the default constructor and then reattaching the initialization arguments. For your particular case, you would define the signature of your newInstance() method (or methods) to take the appropriate number and type of arguments, and then build the arguments bundle appropriately. This is all you want your newInstance() method to do. The callbacks that follow will take care of the rest of the setup of your fragment.

The onInflate() Callback

The next thing that happens is layout view inflation. If your fragment is defined by a <fragment> tag in a layout, your fragment's onInflate() callback will be called. This passes in a reference to the surrounding activity, an AttributeSet with the attributes from the <fragment> tag, and a saved bundle. The saved bundle is the one with the saved state values in it, put there by onSaveInstanceState() if this fragment existed before and is being re-created. The expectation of onInflate() is that you'll read attribute values and save them for later use. At this stage in the fragment's life, it's too early to actually do anything with the user interface. The fragment is not even associated to its activity yet. But that's the next event to occur to your fragment.

The onAttach() Callback

The onAttach() callback is invoked after your fragment is associated with its activity. The activity reference is passed to you if you want to use it. You can at least use the activity to determine information about your enclosing activity. You can also use the activity as a context to do other operations. One thing to note is that the Fragment class has a getActivity() method that will always return the attached activity for your fragment should you need it. Keep in mind that all during this life cycle, the initialization arguments bundle is available to you from the fragment's getArguments()

method. However, once the fragment is attached to its activity, you can't call setArguments() again. Therefore, you can't add to the initialization arguments except in the very beginning.

The onCreate() Callback

Next up is the onCreate() callback. Although this is similar to the activity's onCreate(), the difference is that you should not put code in here that relies on the existence of the activity's view hierarchy. Your fragment may be associated to its activity by now, but you haven't yet been notified that the activity's onCreate() has finished. That's coming up. This callback gets the saved state bundle passed in, if there is one. This callback is about as early as possible to create a background thread to get data that this fragment will need. Your fragment code is running on the UI thread, and you don't want to do disk input/output (I/O) or network accesses on the UI thread. In fact, it makes a lot of sense to fire off a background thread to get things ready. Your background thread is where blocking calls should be. You'll need to hook up with the data later, perhaps using a handler or some other technique.

The onCreateView() Callback

The next callback is onCreateView(). The expectation here is that you will return a view hierarchy for this fragment. The arguments passed into this callback include a LayoutInflater (which you can use to inflate a layout for this fragment), a ViewGroup parent (called *container* in Listing 1-2), and the saved bundle if one exists. It is very important to note that you should not attach the view hierarchy to the ViewGroup parent passed in. That association will happen automatically later. You will very likely get exceptions if you attach the fragment's view hierarchy to the parent in this callback—or at least odd and unexpected application behavior.

Listing 1-2. Creating a Fragment View Hierarchy in on CreateView()

```
@Override
public View onCreateView(LayoutInflater inflater,
                ViewGroup container, Bundle savedInstanceState) {
        if(container == null)
            return null;

        View v = inflater.inflate(R.layout.details, container, false);
        TextView text1 = (TextView) v.findViewById(R.id.text1);
        text1.setText(myDataSet[ getPosition() ] );
        return v;
}
```

The parent is provided so you can use it with the inflate() method of the LayoutInflater. If the parent container value is null, that means this particular fragment won't be viewed because there's no view hierarchy for it to attach to. In this case, you can simply return null from here. Remember that there may be fragments floating around in your application that aren't being displayed. Listing 1-2 shows a sample of what you might want to do in this method.

Here you see how you can access a layout XML file that is just for this fragment and inflate it to a view that you return to the caller. There are several advantages to this approach. You could always construct the view hierarchy in code, but by inflating a layout XML file, you're taking advantage of the system's resource-finding logic. Depending on which configuration the device is in, or for that matter which device you're on, the appropriate layout XML file will be chosen. You can then access a particular view within the layout—in this case, the text1 TextView field—to do what you want with. To repeat a very important point: do not attach the fragment's view to the container parent in this callback. You can see in Listing 1-2 that you use a container in the call to inflate(), but you also pass false for the attachToRoot parameter.

The onViewCreated() Callback

This one is called right after onCreateView() but before any saved state has been put into the UI. The view object passed in is the same view object that got returned from onCreateView().

The onActivityCreated() Callback

You're now getting close to the point where the user can interact with your fragment. The next callback is onActivityCreated(). This is called after the activity has completed its onCreate() callback. You can now trust that the activity's view hierarchy, including your own view hierarchy if you returned one earlier, is ready and available. This is where you can do final tweaks to the user interface before the user sees it. It's also where you can be sure that any other fragment for this activity has been attached to your activity.

The onViewStateRestored() Callback

This one is relatively new, introduced with JellyBean 4.2. Your fragment will have this callback called when the view hierarchy of this fragment has all state restored (if applicable). Previously you had to make decisions in onActivityCreated() about tweaking the UI for a restored fragment. Now you can put that logic in this callback knowing definitely that this fragment is being restored from a saved state.

The onStart() Callback

The next callback in your fragment life cycle is onStart(). Now your fragment is visible to the user. But you haven't started interacting with the user just yet. This callback is tied to the activity's onStart(). As such, whereas previously you may have put your logic into the activity's onStart(), now you're more likely to put your logic into the fragment's onStart(), because that is also where the user interface components are.

The onResume() Callback

The last callback before the user can interact with your fragment is onResume(). This callback is tied to the activity's onResume(). When this callback returns, the user is free to interact with this fragment. For example, if you have a camera preview in your fragment, you would probably enable it in the fragment's onResume().

So now you've reached the point where the app is busily making the user happy. And then the user decides to get out of your app, either by Back'ing out, or by pressing the Home button, or by launching some other application. The next sequence, similar to what happens with an activity, goes in the opposite direction of setting up the fragment for interaction.

The onPause() Callback

The first undo callback on a fragment is onPause(). This callback is tied to the activity's onPause(); just as with an activity, if you have a media player in your fragment or some other shared object, you could pause it, stop it, or give it back via your onPause() method. The same good-citizen rules apply here: you don't want to be playing audio if the user is taking a phone call.

The onSaveInstanceState() Callback

Similar to activities, fragments have an opportunity to save state for later reconstruction. This callback passes in a Bundle object for this fragment to be used as the container for whatever state information you want to hang onto. This is the saved-state bundle passed to the callbacks covered earlier. To prevent memory problems, be careful about what you save into this bundle. Only save what you need. If you need to keep a reference to another fragment, don't try to save or put the other fragment, rather just save the identifier for the other fragment such as its tag or ID. When this fragment runs onViewStateRestored(), then you could re-establish connections to the other fragments that this fragment depends on.

Although you may see this method usually called right after onPause(), the activity to which this fragment belongs calls it when it feels that the fragment's state should be saved. This can occur any time before onDestroy().

The onStop() Callback

The next undo callback is onStop(). This one is tied to the activity's onStop() and serves a purpose similar to an activity's onStop(). A fragment that has been stopped could go straight back to the onStart() callback, which then leads to onResume().

The onDestroyView() Callback

If your fragment is on its way to being killed off or saved, the next callback in the undo direction is onDestroyView(). This will be called after the view hierarchy you created on your onCreateView() callback earlier has been detached from your fragment.

The onDestroy() Callback

Next up is onDestroy(). This is called when the fragment is no longer in use. Note that it is still attached to the activity and is still findable, but it can't do much.

The onDetach() Callback

The final callback in a fragment's life cycle is onDetach(). Once this is invoked, the fragment is not tied to its activity, it does not have a view hierarchy anymore, and all its resources should have been released.

Using setRetainInstance()

You may have noticed the dotted lines in the diagram in Figure 1-2. One of the cool features of a fragment is that you can specify that you don't want the fragment completely destroyed if the activity is being re-created and therefore your fragments will be coming back also. Therefore, Fragment comes with a method called setRetainInstance(), which takes a boolean parameter to tell it "Yes; I want you to hang around when my activity restarts" or "No; go away, and I'll create a new fragment from scratch." A good place to call setRetainInstance() is in the onCreate() callback of a fragment, but in onCreateView() works, as does onActivityCreated().

If the parameter is true, that means you want to keep your fragment object in memory and not start over from scratch. However, if your activity is going away and being re-created, you'll have to detach your fragment from this activity and attach it to the new one. The bottom line is that if the retain instance value is true, you won't actually destroy your fragment instance, and therefore you won't need to create a new one on the other side. The dotted lines on the diagram mean you would skip the onDestroy() callback on the way out, you'd skip the onCreate() callback when your fragment is being re-attached to your new activity, and all other callbacks would fire. Because an activity is re-created most likely for configuration changes, your fragment callbacks should probably assume that the configuration has changed, and therefore should take appropriate action. This would include inflating the layout to create a new view hierarchy in onCreateView(), for example. The code provided in Listing 1-2 would take care of that as it is written. If you choose to use the retain-instance feature, you may decide not to put some of your initialization logic in onCreate() because it won't always get called the way the other callbacks will.

Sample Fragment App Showing the Life Cycle

There's nothing like seeing a real example to get an appreciation for a concept. You'll use a sample application that has been instrumented so you can see all these callbacks in action. You're going to work with a sample application that uses a list of Shakespearean titles in one fragment; when the user clicks one of the titles, some text from that play will appear in a separate fragment. This sample application will work in both landscape and portrait modes on a tablet. Then you'll configure it to run as if on a smaller screen so you can see how to separate the text fragment into an activity. You'll start with the XML layout of your activity in landscape mode in Listing 1-3, which will look like Figure 1-3 when it runs.

Listing 1-3. Your Activity's Layout XML for Landscape Mode

```
<?xml version="1.0" encoding="utf-8"?>
<!-- This file is res/layout-land/main.xml -->
<LinearLayout xmlns:android="http://schemas.android.com/apk/res/android"
        android:orientation="horizontal"
        android:layout_width="match_parent"
        android:layout_height="match_parent">

    <fragment class="com.androidbook.fragments.bard.TitlesFragment"
            android:id="@+id/titles" android:layout_weight="1"
            android:layout_width="0px"
            android:layout_height="match_parent" />
```

```
<FrameLayout
        android:id="@+id/details" android:layout_weight="2"
        android:layout_width="0px"
        android:layout_height="match_parent" />

</LinearLayout>
```

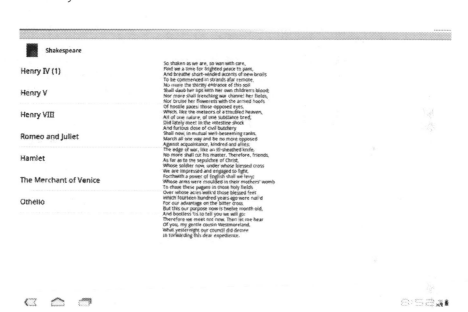

Figure 1-3. The user interface of your sample fragment application

> **Note**   At the end of the chapter is the URL you can use to download the
> projects in this chapter. This will allow you to import these projects into
> your IDE (such as Eclipse or Android Studio) directly.

This layout looks like a lot of other layouts you've seen throughout the book, horizontally left to right with two main objects. There's a special new tag, though, called <fragment>, and this tag has a new attribute called class. Keep in mind that a fragment is not a view, so the layout XML is a little different for a fragment than it is for everything else. The other thing to keep in mind is that the <fragment> tag is just a placeholder in this layout. You should not put child tags under <fragment> in a layout XML file.

The other attributes for a fragment look familiar and serve a purpose similar to that for a view. The fragment tag's class attribute specifies your extended class for the titles of your application. That is, you must extend one of the Android Fragment classes to implement your logic, and the <fragment> tag must know the name of your extended class. A fragment has its own view hierarchy that will be created later by the fragment itself. The next tag is a FrameLayout—not another <fragment> tag. Why is that? We'll explain in more detail later, but for now, you should be aware that you're going to be doing some transitions on the text, swapping out one fragment with another. You use the FrameLayout as the view container to hold the current text fragment. With your titles fragment, you have one—and only one—fragment to worry about: no swapping and no transitions. For the area that displays the Shakespearean text, you'll have several fragments.

The MainActivity Java code is in Listing 1-4. Actually, the listing only shows the interesting code. The code is instrumented with logging messages so you can see what's going on through LogCat. Please review the source code files for ShakespeareInstrumented from the web site to see all of it.

Listing 1-4. Interesting Source Code from MainActivity

```java
public boolean isMultiPane() {
    return getResources().getConfiguration().orientation
            == Configuration.ORIENTATION_LANDSCAPE;
}

/**
 * Helper function to show the details of a selected item, either by
 * displaying a fragment in-place in the current UI, or starting a
 * whole new activity in which it is displayed.
 */
public void showDetails(int index) {
    Log.v(TAG, "in MainActivity showDetails(" + index + ")");

    if (isMultiPane()) {
        // Check what fragment is shown, replace if needed.
        DetailsFragment details = (DetailsFragment)
                getFragmentManager().findFragmentById(R.id.details);
        if ( (details == null) ||
             (details.getShownIndex() != index) ) {
            // Make new fragment to show this selection.
            details = DetailsFragment.newInstance(index);
```

```
                // Execute a transaction, replacing any existing
                // fragment with this one inside the frame.
                Log.v(TAG, "about to run FragmentTransaction...");
                FragmentTransaction ft
                        = getFragmentManager().beginTransaction();
                ft.setTransition(
                        FragmentTransaction.TRANSIT_FRAGMENT_FADE);
                //ft.addToBackStack("details");
                ft.replace(R.id.details, details);
                ft.commit();
            }

        } else {
            // Otherwise you need to launch a new activity to display
            // the dialog fragment with selected text.
            Intent intent = new Intent();
            intent.setClass(this, DetailsActivity.class);
            intent.putExtra("index", index);
            startActivity(intent);
        }
    }
}
```

This is a very simple activity to write. To determine multipane mode (that is, whether you need to use fragments side by side), you just use the orientation of the device. If you're in landscape mode, you're multipane; if you're in portrait mode, you're not. The helper method showDetails() is there to figure out how to show the text when a title is selected. The index is the position of the title in the title list. If you're in multipane mode, you're going to use a fragment to show the text. You're calling this fragment a DetailsFragment, and you use a factory-type method to create one with the index. The interesting code for the DetailsFragment class is shown in Listing 1-5 (minus all of the logging code). As we did before in TitlesFragment, the various callbacks of DetailsFragment have logging added so we can watch what happens via LogCat. You'll come back to your showDetails() method later.

Listing 1-5. Source Code for DetailsFragment

```
public class DetailsFragment extends Fragment {

    private int mIndex = 0;

    public static DetailsFragment newInstance(int index) {
        Log.v(MainActivity.TAG, "in DetailsFragment newInstance(" +
                                index + ")");
```

```
        DetailsFragment df = new DetailsFragment();

        // Supply index input as an argument.
        Bundle args = new Bundle();
        args.putInt("index", index);
        df.setArguments(args);
        return df;
    }

    public static DetailsFragment newInstance(Bundle bundle) {
        int index = bundle.getInt("index", 0);
        return newInstance(index);
    }

    @Override
    public void onCreate(Bundle myBundle) {
        Log.v(MainActivity.TAG,
                "in DetailsFragment onCreate. Bundle contains:");
        if(myBundle != null) {
            for(String key : myBundle.keySet()) {
                Log.v(MainActivity.TAG, "    " + key);
            }
        }
        else {
            Log.v(MainActivity.TAG, "    myBundle is null");
        }
        super.onCreate(myBundle);

        mIndex = getArguments().getInt("index", 0);
    }

    public int getShownIndex() {
        return mIndex;
    }

    @Override
    public View onCreateView(LayoutInflater inflater,
            ViewGroup container, Bundle savedInstanceState) {
        Log.v(MainActivity.TAG,
                "in DetailsFragment onCreateView. container = " +
                container);

        // Don't tie this fragment to anything through the inflater.
        // Android takes care of attaching fragments for us. The
        // container is only passed in so you can know about the
        // container where this View hierarchy is going to go.
        View v = inflater.inflate(R.layout.details, container, false);
```

```
        TextView text1 = (TextView) v.findViewById(R.id.text1);
        text1.setText(Shakespeare.DIALOGUE[ mIndex ] );
        return v;
    }
}
```

The DetailsFragment class is actually fairly simple as well. Now you can see how to instantiate this fragment. It's important to point out that you're instantiating this fragment in code because your layout defines the ViewGroup container (a FrameLayout) that your details fragment is going to go into. Because the fragment is not itself defined in the layout XML for the activity, as your titles fragment was, you need to instantiate your details fragments in code.

To create a new details fragment, you use your newInstance() method. As discussed earlier, this factory method invokes the default constructor and then sets the arguments bundle with the value of index. Once newInstance() has run, your details fragment can retrieve the value of index in any of its callbacks by referring to the arguments bundle via getArguments(). For your convenience, in onCreate() you can save the index value from the arguments bundle to a member field in your DetailsFragment class.

You might wonder why you didn't simply set the mIndex value in newInstance(). The reason is that Android will, behind the scenes, re-create your fragment using the default constructor. Then it sets the arguments bundle to what it was before. Android won't use your newInstance() method, so the only reliable way to ensure that mIndex is set is to read the value from the arguments bundle and set it in onCreate(). The convenience method getShownIndex() retrieves the value of that index. Now the only method left to describe in the details fragment is onCreateView(). And this is very simple, too.

The purpose of onCreateView() is to return the view hierarchy for your fragment. Remember that based on your configuration, you could want all kinds of different layouts for this fragment. Therefore, the most common thing to do is utilize a layout XML file for your fragment. In your sample application, you specify the layout for the fragment to be details.xml using the resource R.layout.details. The XML for details.xml is in Listing 1-6.

Listing 1-6. The details.xml Layout File for the Details Fragment

```
<?xml version="1.0" encoding="utf-8"?>
<!-- This file is res/layout/details.xml -->
<LinearLayout
    xmlns:android="http://schemas.android.com/apk/res/android"
    android:layout_width="match_parent"
    android:layout_height="match_parent">
```

```
<ScrollView android:id="@+id/scroller"
    android:layout_width="match_parent"
    android:layout_height="match_parent">
  <TextView android:id="@+id/text1"
      android:layout_width="match_parent"
      android:layout_height="match_parent" />
</ScrollView>
</LinearLayout>
```

For your sample application, you can use the exact same layout file for details whether you're in landscape mode or in portrait mode. This layout is not for the activity, it's just for your fragment to display the text. Because it could be considered the default layout, you can store it in the /res/layout directory and it will be found and used even if you're in landscape mode. When Android goes looking for the details XML file, it tries the specific directories that closely match the device's configuration, but it will end up in the /res/layout directory if it can't find the details.xml file in any of the other places. Of course, if you want to have a different layout for your fragment in landscape mode, you could define a separate details.xml layout file and store it under /res/layout-land. Feel free to experiment with different details.xml files.

When your details fragment's onCreateView() is called, you will simply grab the appropriate details.xml layout file, inflate it, and set the text to the text from the Shakespeare class. The entire Java code for Shakespeare is not shown here, but a portion is in Listing 1-7 so you understand how it was done. For the complete source, access the project download files, as described in the "References" section at the end of this chapter.

Listing 1-7. Source Code for Shakespeare.java

```
public class Shakespeare {
    public static String TITLES[] = {
            "Henry IV (1)",
            "Henry V",
            "Henry VIII",
            "Romeo and Juliet",
            "Hamlet",
            "The Merchant of Venice",
            "Othello"
    };
    public static String DIALOGUE[] = {
        "So shaken as we are, so wan with care,\n...
... and so on ...
```

Now your details fragment view hierarchy contains the text from the selected title. Your details fragment is ready to go. And you can return to MainActivity's showDetails() method to talk about FragmentTransactions.

FragmentTransactions and the Fragment Back Stack

The code in showDetails() that pulls in your new details fragment (partially shown again in Listing 1-8) looks rather simple, but there's a lot going on here. It's worth spending some time to explain what is happening and why. If your activity is in multipane mode, you want to show the details in a fragment next to the title list. You may already be showing details, which means you may have a details fragment visible to the user. Either way, the resource ID R.id.details is for the FrameLayout for your activity, as shown in Listing 1-3. If you have a details fragment sitting in the layout because you didn't assign any other ID to it, it will have this ID. Therefore, to find out if there's a details fragment in the layout, you can ask the fragment manager using findFragmentById(). This will return null if the frame layout is empty or will give you the current details fragment. You can then decide if you need to place a new details fragment in the layout, either because the layout is empty or because there's a details fragment for some other title. Once you make the determination to create and use a new details fragment, you invoke the factory method to create a new instance of a details fragment. Now you can put this new fragment into place for the user to see.

Listing 1-8. Fragment Transaction Example

```
public void showDetails(int index) {
    Log.v(TAG, "in MainActivity showDetails(" + index + ")");

    if (isMultiPane()) {
        // Check what fragment is shown, replace if needed.
        DetailsFragment details = (DetailsFragment)
                getFragmentManager().findFragmentById(R.id.details);
        if (details == null || details.getShownIndex() != index) {
            // Make new fragment to show this selection.
            details = DetailsFragment.newInstance(index);

            // Execute a transaction, replacing any existing
            // fragment with this one inside the frame.
            Log.v(TAG, "about to run FragmentTransaction...");
            FragmentTransaction ft
                    = getFragmentManager().beginTransaction();
            ft.setTransition(
                    FragmentTransaction.TRANSIT_FRAGMENT_FADE);
```

```
        //ft.addToBackStack("details");
        ft.replace(R.id.details, details);
        ft.commit();
    }
        // The rest was left out to save space.
}
```

A key concept to understand is that a fragment must live inside a view container, also known as a *view group*. The ViewGroup class includes such things as layouts and their derived classes. FrameLayout is a good choice as the container for the details fragment in the main.xml layout file of your activity. A FrameLayout is simple, and all you need is a simple container for your fragment, without the extra baggage that comes with other types of layouts. The FrameLayout is where your details fragment is going to go. If you had instead specified another <fragment> tag in the activity's layout file instead of a FrameLayout, you would not be able to replace the current fragment with a new fragment (i.e., swap fragments).

The FragmentTransaction is what you use to do your swapping. You tell the fragment transaction that you want to replace whatever is in your frame layout with your new details fragment. You could have avoided all this by locating the resource ID of the details TextView and just setting the text of it to the new text for the new Shakespeare title. But there's another side to fragments that explains why you use FragmentTransactions.

As you know, activities are arranged in a stack, and as you get deeper and deeper into an application, it's not uncommon to have a stack of several activities going at once. When you press the Back button, the topmost activity goes away, and you are returned to the activity below, which resumes for you. This can continue until you're at the home screen again.

This was fine when an activity was just single-purpose, but now that an activity can have several fragments going at once, and because you can go deeper into your application without leaving the topmost activity, Android really needed to extend the Back button stack concept to include fragments as well. In fact, fragments demand this even more. When there are several fragments interacting with each other at the same time in an activity, and there's a transition to new content across several fragments at once, pressing the Back button should cause each of the fragments to roll back one step *together*. To ensure that each fragment properly participates in the rollback, a FragmentTransaction is created and managed to perform that coordination.

Be aware that a back stack for fragments is not required within an activity. You can code your application to let the Back button work at the activity level and not at the fragment level at all. If there's no back stack for your fragments, pressing the Back button will pop the current activity off the stack and return the user to whatever was underneath. If you choose to take advantage of the back stack for fragments, you will want to uncomment in Listing 1-8 the line that says ft.addToBackStack("details"). For this particular case, you've hardcoded the tag parameter to be the string "details". This tag should be an appropriate string name that represents the state of the fragments at the time of the transaction. The tag is not necessarily a name for a specific fragment but rather for the fragment transaction and all the fragments in the transaction. You will be able to interrogate the back stack in code using the tag value to delete entries, as well as pop entries off. You will want meaningful tags on these transactions to be able to find the appropriate ones later.

Fragment Transaction Transitions and Animations

One of the very nice things about fragment transactions is that you can perform transitions from an old fragment to a new fragment using transitions and animations. Let's use a fragment transaction transition to add special effects when you swap out the old details fragment with a new details fragment. This can add polish to your application, making the switch from the old to the new fragment look smooth.

One method to accomplish this is setTransition(), as shown in Listing 1-8. However, there are a few different transitions available. You used a fade in your example, but you can also use the setCustomAnimations() method to describe other special effects, such as sliding one fragment out to the right as another slides in from the left. The custom animations use the new object animation definitions, not the old ones. The old anim XML files use tags such as <translate>, whereas the new XML files use <objectAnimator>. The old standard XML files are located in the /data/res/anim directory under the appropriate Android SDK platforms directory (such as platforms/ android-11 for Honeycomb). There are some new XML files located in the /data/res/animator directory here, too. Your code could be something like

```
ft.setCustomAnimations(android.R.animator.fade_in, android.R.animator.
fade_out);
```

which will cause the new fragment to fade in as the old fragment fades out. The first parameter applies to the fragment entering, and the second parameter applies to the fragment exiting. Feel free to explore the Android animator directory for more stock animations. The other very important bit of knowledge you need is that the transition calls need to come before the replace() call; otherwise, they will have no effect.

Using the object animator for special effects on fragments can be a fun way to do transitions. There are two other methods on FragmentTransaction you should know about: hide() and show(). Both of these methods take a fragment as a parameter, and they do exactly what you'd expect. For a fragment in the fragment manager associated to a view container, the methods simply hide or show the fragment in the user interface. The fragment does not get removed from the fragment manager in the process, but it certainly must be tied into a view container in order to affect its visibility. If a fragment does not have a view hierarchy, or if its view hierarchy is not tied into the displayed view hierarchy, then these methods won't do anything.

Once you've specified the special effects for your fragment transaction, you have to tell it the main work that you want done. In your case, you're replacing whatever is in the frame layout with your new details fragment. That's where the replace() method comes in. This is equivalent to calling remove() for any fragments that are already in the frame layout and then add() for your new details fragment, which means you could just call remove() or add() as needed instead.

The final action you must take when working with a fragment transaction is to commit it. The commit() method does not cause things to happen immediately but rather schedules the work for when the UI thread is ready to do it.

Now you should understand why you need to go to so much trouble to change the content in a simple fragment. It's not just that you want to change the text; you might want a special graphics effect during the transition. You may also want to save the transition details in a fragment transaction that you can reverse later. That last point may be confusing, so we'll clarify.

This is not a transaction in the truest sense of the word. When you pop fragment transactions off the back stack, you are not undoing all the data changes that may have taken place. If data changed within your activity, for example, as you created fragment transactions on the back stack, pressing the Back button does not cause the activity data changes to revert back to their previous values. You are merely stepping back through the user interface views the way you came in, just as you do with activities, but in this case it's for fragments. Because of the way fragments are saved and restored, the inner state of a fragment that has been restored from a saved state will depend on what values you saved with the fragment and how you manage to restore them. So your fragments may look the same as they did previously but your activity will not, unless you take steps to restore activity state when you restore fragments.

In your example, you're only working with one view container and bringing in one details fragment. If your user interface were more complicated, you could manipulate other fragments within the fragment transaction. What you are actually doing is beginning the transaction, replacing any existing fragment in your details frame layout with your new details fragment, specifying a fade-in animation, and committing the transaction. You commented out the part where this transaction is added to the back stack, but you could certainly uncomment it to take part in the back stack.

The FragmentManager

The FragmentManager is a component that takes care of the fragments belonging to an activity. This includes fragments on the back stack and fragments that may just be hanging around. We'll explain.

Fragments should only be created within the context of an activity. This occurs either through the inflation of an activity's layout XML or through direct instantiation using code like that in Listing 1-1. When instantiated through code, a fragment usually gets attached to the activity using a fragment transaction. In either case, the FragmentManager class is used to access and manage these fragments for an activity.

You use the getFragmentManager() method on either an activity or an attached fragment to retrieve a fragment manager. You saw in Listing 1-8 that a fragment manager is where you get a fragment transaction. Besides getting a fragment transaction, you can also get a fragment using the fragment's ID, its tag, or a combination of bundle and key. The fragment's ID will either be the fragment's resource ID if the fragment was inflated from XML, or it will be the container's resource ID if the fragment was placed into a view using a fragment transaction. A fragment's tag is a String that you can assign in the fragment's XML definition, or when the fragment is placed in a view via a fragment transaction. The bundle and key method of retrieving a fragment only works for fragments that were persisted using the putFragment() method.

For getting a fragment, the getter methods include findFragmentById(), findFragmentByTag(), and getFragment(). The getFragment() method would be used in conjunction with putFragment(), which also takes a bundle, a key, and the fragment to be put. The bundle is most likely going to be the savedState bundle, and putFragment() will be used in the onSaveInstanceState() callback to save the state of the current activity (or another fragment). The getFragment() method would probably be called in onCreate() to correspond to putFragment(), although for a fragment, the bundle is available to the other callback methods, as described earlier.

Obviously, you can't use the getFragmentManager() method on a fragment that has not been attached to an activity yet. But it's also true that you can attach a fragment to an activity without making it visible to the user yet. If you do this, you should associate a String tag to the fragment so you can get to it in the future. You'd most likely use this method of FragmentTransaction to do this:

```
public FragmentTransaction add (Fragment fragment, String tag)
```

In fact, you can have a fragment that does not exhibit a view hierarchy. This might be done to encapsulate certain logic together such that it could be attached to an activity, yet still retain some autonomy from the activity's life cycle and from other fragments. When an activity goes through a re-create cycle due to a device-configuration change, this non-UI fragment could remain largely intact while the activity goes away and comes back again. This would be a good candidate for the setRetainInstance() option.

The fragment back stack is also the domain of the fragment manager. Whereas a fragment transaction is used to put fragments onto the back stack, the fragment manager can take fragments off the back stack. This is usually done using the fragment's ID or tag, but it can be done based on position in the back stack or just to pop the topmost fragment.

Finally, the fragment manager has methods for some debugging features, such as turning on debugging messages to LogCat using enableDebugLogging() or dumping the current state of the fragment manager to a stream using dump(). Note that you turned on fragment manager debugging in the onCreate() method of your activity in Listing 1-4.

Caution When Referencing Fragments

It's time to revisit the earlier discussion of the fragment's life cycle and the arguments and saved-state bundles. Android could save one of your fragments at many different times. This means that at the moment your application wants to retrieve that fragment, it's possible that it is not in memory. For this reason, we caution you *not* to think that a variable reference to a fragment is going to remain valid for a long time. If fragments are being replaced in a container view using fragment transactions, any reference to the old fragment is now pointing to a fragment that is possibly on the back stack. Or a fragment may get detached from the activity's view hierarchy during an application configuration change such as a screen rotation. Be careful.

If you're going to hold onto a reference to a fragment, be aware of when it could get saved away; when you need to find it again, use one of the getter methods of the fragment manager. If you want to hang onto a fragment reference, such as when an activity is going through a configuration change, you can use the putFragment() method with the appropriate bundle. In the case of both activities and fragments, the appropriate bundle is the savedState bundle that is used in onSaveInstanceState() and that reappears in onCreate() (or, in the case of fragments, the other early callbacks of the fragment's life cycle). You will probably never store a direct fragment reference into the arguments bundle of a fragment; if you're tempted to do so, please think very carefully about it first.

The other way you can get to a specific fragment is by querying for it using a known tag or known ID. The getter methods described previously will allow retrieval of fragments from the fragment manager this way, which means you have the option of just remembering the tag or ID of a fragment so that you can retrieve it from the fragment manager using one of those values, as opposed to using putFragment() and getFragment().

Saving Fragment State

Another interesting class was introduced in Android 3.2: Fragment.SavedState. Using the saveFragmentInstanceState() method of FragmentManager, you can pass this method a fragment, and it returns an object representing the state of that fragment. You can then use that object when initializing a fragment, using Fragment's setInitialSavedState() method. Chapter 2 discusses this in more detail.

ListFragments and <fragment>

There are still a few more things to cover to make your sample application complete. The first is the TitlesFragment class. This is the one that is created via the main.xml file of your main activity. The <fragment> tag serves as your placeholder for where this fragment will go and does not define what the view hierarchy will look like for this fragment. The interesting code for your TitlesFragment is in Listing 1-9. For all of the code please refer to the source code files. TitlesFragment displays the list of titles for your application.

Listing 1-9. TitlesFragment Java Code

```java
public class TitlesFragment extends ListFragment {
    private MainActivity myActivity = null;
    int mCurCheckPosition = 0;

    @Override
    public void onAttach(Activity myActivity) {
        Log.v(MainActivity.TAG,
            "in TitlesFragment onAttach; activity is: " + myActivity);
        super.onAttach(myActivity);
        this.myActivity = (MainActivity)myActivity;
    }

    @Override
    public void onActivityCreated(Bundle savedState) {
        Log.v(MainActivity.TAG,
            "in TitlesFragment onActivityCreated. savedState contains:");
        if(savedState != null) {
            for(String key : savedState.keySet()) {
                Log.v(MainActivity.TAG, "    " + key);
            }
        }
        else {
            Log.v(MainActivity.TAG, "    savedState is null");
        }
        super.onActivityCreated(savedState);

        // Populate list with your static array of titles.
        setListAdapter(new ArrayAdapter<String>(getActivity(),
                android.R.layout.simple_list_item_1,
                Shakespeare.TITLES));

        if (savedState != null) {
            // Restore last state for checked position.
            mCurCheckPosition = savedState.getInt("curChoice", 0);
        }

        // Get your ListFragment's ListView and update it
        ListView lv = getListView();
        lv.setChoiceMode(ListView.CHOICE_MODE_SINGLE);
        lv.setSelection(mCurCheckPosition);

        // Activity is created, fragments are available
        // Go ahead and populate the details fragment
        myActivity.showDetails(mCurCheckPosition);
    }
```

```
    @Override
    public void onSaveInstanceState(Bundle outState) {
        Log.v(MainActivity.TAG, "in TitlesFragment onSaveInstanceState");
        super.onSaveInstanceState(outState);
        outState.putInt("curChoice", mCurCheckPosition);
    }

    @Override
    public void onListItemClick(ListView l, View v, int pos, long id) {
        Log.v(MainActivity.TAG,
            "in TitlesFragment onListItemClick. pos = "
            + pos);
        myActivity.showDetails(pos);
        mCurCheckPosition = pos;
    }

    @Override
    public void onDetach() {
        Log.v(MainActivity.TAG, "in TitlesFragment onDetach");
        super.onDetach();
        myActivity = null;
    }
}
```

Unlike DetailsFragment, for this fragment you don't do anything in the onCreateView() callback. This is because you're extending the ListFragment class, which contains a ListView already. The default onCreateView() for a ListFragment creates this ListView for you and returns it. It's not until onActivityCreated() that you do any real application logic. By this time in your application, you can be sure that the activity's view hierarchy, plus this fragment's, has been created. The resource ID for that ListView is android.R.id.list1, but you can always call getListView() if you need to get a reference to it, which you do in onActivityCreated(). Because ListFragment manages the ListView, do not attach the adapter to the ListView directly. You must use the ListFragment's setListAdapter() method instead. The activity's view hierarchy is now set up, so you're safe going back into the activity to do the showDetails() call.

At this point in your sample activity's life, you've added a list adapter to your list view, you've restored the current position (if you came back from a restore, due perhaps to a configuration change), and you've asked the activity (in showDetails()) to set the text to correspond to the selected Shakespearean title.

Your TitlesFragment class also has a listener on the list so when the user clicks another title, the onListItemClick() callback is called, and you switch the text to correspond to that title, again using the showDetails() method.

Another difference between this fragment and the earlier details fragment is that when this fragment is being destroyed and re-created, you save state in a bundle (the value of the current position in the list), and you read it back in onCreate(). Unlike the details fragments that get swapped in and out of the FrameLayout on your activity's layout, there is just one titles fragment to think about. So when there is a configuration change and your titles fragment is going through a save-and-restore operation, you want to remember where you were. With the details fragments, you can re-create them without having to remember the previous state.

Invoking a Separate Activity When Needed

There's a piece of code we haven't talked about yet, and that is in showDetails() when you're in portrait mode and the details fragment won't fit properly on the same page as the titles fragment. If the screen real estate won't permit feasible viewing of a fragment that would otherwise be shown alongside the other fragments, you will need to launch a separate activity to show the user interface of that fragment. For your sample application, you implement a details activity; the code is in Listing 1-10.

Listing 1-10. Showing a New Activity When a Fragment Doesn't Fit

```
public class DetailsActivity extends Activity {

    @Override
    public void onCreate(Bundle savedInstanceState) {
        Log.v(MainActivity.TAG, "in DetailsActivity onCreate");
        super.onCreate(savedInstanceState);

        if (getResources().getConfiguration().orientation
                == Configuration.ORIENTATION_LANDSCAPE) {
            // If the screen is now in landscape mode, it means
            // that your MainActivity is being shown with both
            // the titles and the text, so this activity is
            // no longer needed. Bail out and let the MainActivity
            // do all the work.
            finish();
            return;
        }

        if(getIntent() != null) {
            // This is another way to instantiate a details
            // fragment.
            DetailsFragment details =
                DetailsFragment.newInstance(getIntent().getExtras());
```

```
        getFragmentManager().beginTransaction()
            .add(android.R.id.content, details)
            .commit();
    }
  }
}
```

There are several interesting aspects to this code. For one thing, it is really easy to implement. You make a simple determination of the device's orientation, and as long as you're in portrait mode, you set up a new details fragment within this details activity. If you're in landscape mode, your MainActivity is able to display both the titles fragment and the details fragment, so there is no reason to be displaying this activity at all. You may wonder why you would ever launch this activity if you're in landscape mode, and the answer is, you wouldn't. However, once this activity has been started in portrait mode, if the user rotates the device to landscape mode, this details activity will get restarted due to the configuration change. So now the activity is starting up, and it's in landscape mode. At that moment, it makes sense to finish this activity and let the MainActivity take over and do all the work.

Another interesting aspect about this details activity is that you never set the root content view using setContentView(). So how does the user interface get created? If you look carefully at the add() method call on the fragment transaction, you will see that the view container to which you add the fragment is specified as the resource android.R.id.content. This is the top-level view container for an activity, and therefore when you attach your fragment view hierarchy to this container, your fragment view hierarchy becomes the only view hierarchy for the activity. You used the very same DetailsFragment class as before with the other newInstance() method to create the fragment (the one that takes a bundle as a parameter), then you simply attached it to the top of the activity's view hierarchy. This causes the fragment to be displayed within this new activity.

From the user's point of view, they are now looking at just the details fragment view, which is the text from the Shakespearean play. If the user wants to select a different title, they press the Back button, which pops this activity to reveal your main activity (with the titles fragment only). The other choice for the user is to rotate the device to get back to landscape mode. Then your details activity will call finish() and go away, revealing the also-rotated main activity underneath.

When the device is in portrait mode, if you're not showing the details fragment in your main activity, you should have a separate main.xml layout file for portrait mode like the one in Listing 1-11.

Listing 1-11. The Layout for a Portrait Main Activity

```xml
<?xml version="1.0" encoding="utf-8"?>
<!-- This file is res/layout/main.xml -->
<LinearLayout xmlns:android="http://schemas.android.com/apk/res/android"
        android:orientation="vertical"
        android:layout_width="match_parent"
        android:layout_height="match_parent">

    <fragment class="com.androidbook.fragments.bard.TitlesFragment"
            android:id="@+id/titles"
            android:layout_width="match_parent"
            android:layout_height="match_parent" />

</LinearLayout>
```

Of course, you could make this layout whatever you want it to be. For your purposes here, you simply make it show the titles fragment by itself. It's very nice that your titles fragment class doesn't need to include much code to deal with the device reconfiguration.

Take a moment to view this application's manifest file. In it you find the main activity with a category of LAUNCHER so that it will appear in the device's list of apps. Then you have the separate DetailsActivity with a category of DEFAULT. This allows you to start the details activity from code but will not show the details activity as an app in the App list.

Persistence of Fragments

When you play with this sample application, make sure you rotate the device (pressing Ctrl+F11 rotates the device in the emulator). You will see that the device rotates, and the fragments rotate right along with it. If you watch the LogCat messages, you will see a lot of them for this application. In particular, during a device rotation, pay careful attention to the messages about fragments; not only does the activity get destroyed and re-created, but the fragments do also.

So far, you only wrote a tiny bit of code on the titles fragment to remember the current position in the titles list across restarts. You didn't do anything in the details fragment code to handle reconfigurations, and that's because you didn't need to. Android will take care of hanging onto the fragments that are in the fragment manager, saving them away, then restoring them when the activity is being re-created. You should realize that the fragments you get back after the reconfiguration is complete are very likely not the same fragments in memory that you had before. These fragments have been reconstructed for you. Android saved the arguments bundle and the knowledge of which type of fragment it was, and it stored the saved-state bundles for each fragment that contain saved-state information about the fragment to use to restore it on the other side.

The LogCat messages show you the fragments going through their life cycles in sync with the activity. You will see that your details fragment gets re-created, but your newInstance() method does not get called again. Instead, Android uses the default constructor, attaches the arguments bundle to it, and then starts calling the callbacks on the fragment. This is why it is so important not to do anything fancy in the newInstance() method: when the fragment gets re-created, it won't do it through newInstance().

You should also appreciate by now that you've been able to reuse your fragments in a few different places. The titles fragment was used in two different layouts, but if you look at the titles fragment code, it doesn't worry about the attributes of each layout. You could make the layouts rather different from each other, and the titles fragment code would look the same. The same can be said of the details fragment. It was used in your main landscape layout and within the details activity all by itself. Again, the layout for the details fragment could have been very different between the two, and the code of the details fragment would be the same. The code of the details activity was very simple, also.

So far, you've explored two of the fragment types: the base Fragment class and the ListFragment subclass. Fragment has other subclasses: the DialogFragment, PreferenceFragment, and WebViewFragment. We'll cover DialogFragment and PreferenceFragment in Chapters 3 and 4, respectively.

Communications with Fragments

Because the fragment manager knows about all fragments attached to the current activity, the activity or any fragment in that activity can ask for any other fragment using the getter methods described earlier. Once the fragment reference has been obtained, the activity or fragment could cast the reference appropriately and then call methods directly on that activity or fragment. This would cause your fragments to have more knowledge about the other fragments than might normally be desired, but don't forget that you're running this application on a mobile device, so cutting corners can sometimes be justified. A code snippet is provided in Listing 1-12 to show how one fragment might communicate directly with another fragment. The snippet would be part of one of your extended Fragment classes, and FragmentOther is a different extended Fragment class.

Listing 1-12. Direct Fragment-to-Fragment Communication

```
FragmentOther fragOther =
        (FragmentOther)getFragmentManager().findFragmentByTag("other");
fragOther.callCustomMethod( arg1, arg2 );
```

In Listing 1-12, the current fragment has direct knowledge of the class of the other fragment and also which methods exist on that class. This may be okay because these fragments are part of one application, and it can be easier to simply accept the fact that some fragments will know about other fragments. We'll show you a cleaner way to communicate between fragments in the DialogFragment sample application in Chapter 3.

Using startActivity() and setTargetFragment()

A feature of fragments that is very much like activities is the ability of a fragment to start an activity. Fragment has a startActivity() method and startActivityForResult() method. These work just like the ones for activities; when a result is passed back, it will cause the onActivityResult() callback to fire on the fragment that started the activity.

There's another communication mechanism you should know about. When one fragment wants to start another fragment, there is a feature that lets the calling fragment set its identity with the called fragment. Listing 1-13 shows an example of what it might look like.

Listing 1-13. Fragment-to-Target-Fragment Setup

```
mCalledFragment = new CalledFragment();
mCalledFragment.setTargetFragment(this, 0);
fm.beginTransaction().add(mCalledFragment, "work").commit();
```

With these few lines, you've created a new CalledFragment object, set the target fragment on the called fragment to the current fragment, and added the called fragment to the fragment manager and activity using a fragment transaction. When the called fragment starts to run, it will be able to call getTargetFragment(), which will return a reference to the calling fragment. With this reference, the called fragment could invoke methods on the calling fragment or even access view components directly. For example, in Listing 1-14, the called fragment could set text in the UI of the calling fragment directly.

Listing 1-14. Target Fragment-to-Fragment Communication

```
TextView tv = (TextView)
    getTargetFragment().getView().findViewById(R.id.text1);
tv.setText("Set from the called fragment");
```

References

Here are some helpful references to topics you may wish to explore further:

- www.androidbook.com/androidfragments/projects: A list of downloadable projects related to this book. The file called AndroidFragments_Ch01_Fragments.zip contains all projects from this chapter, listed in separate root directories. There is also a README.TXT file that describes exactly how to import projects into an IDE from one of these zip files. It includes some projects that use the Fragment Compatibility SDK for older Androids as well.

- http://developer.android.com/guide/components/fragments.html: The Android Developer's Guide page to fragments.

- http://developer.android.com/design/patterns/multi-pane-layouts.html: Android design guidelines for multipane layouts.

- http://developer.android.com/training/basics/fragments/index.html: Android training page for fragments.

Summary

This chapter introduced the Fragment class and its related classes for the manager, transactions, and subclasses. This is a summary of what's been covered in this chapter:

- The Fragment class, what it does, and how to use it.

- Why fragments cannot be used without being attached to one and only one activity.

- That although fragments can be instantiated with a static factory method such as newInstance(), you must always have a default constructor and a way to save initialization values into an initialization arguments bundle.

- The life cycle of a fragment and how it is intertwined with the life cycle of the activity that owns the fragment.

- `FragmentManager` and its features.

- Managing device configurations using fragments.

- Combining fragments into a single activity, or splitting them between multiple activities.

- Using fragment transactions to change what's displayed to a user, and animating those transitions using cool effects.

- New behaviors that are possible with the Back button when using fragments.

- Using the `<fragment>` tag in a layout.

- Using a `FrameLayout` as a placeholder for a fragment when you want to use transitions.

- `ListFragment` and how to use an adapter to populate the data (very much like a `ListView`).

- Launching a new activity when a fragment can't fit onto the current screen, and how to adjust when a configuration change makes it possible to see multiple fragments again.

- Communicating between fragments, and between a fragment and its activity.

Chapter 2

Responding to Configuration Changes

When an application is running on a device, and the device's configuration changes (for example, is rotated 90 degrees), your application needs to respond accordingly. The new configuration will most likely look different from the previous configuration. For example, switching from portrait to landscape mode means the screen went from being tall and narrow to being short and wide. The UI elements (buttons, text, lists, and so on) will need to be rearranged, resized, or even removed to accommodate the new configuration.

In Android, a configuration change by default causes the current activity to go away and be re-created. The application itself keeps on running, but it has the opportunity to change how the activity is displayed in response to the configuration change. In the rare case that you need to handle a configuration change without destroying and re-creating your activity, Android provides a way to handle that as well.

Be aware that configuration changes can take on many forms, not just device rotation. If a device gets connected to a dock, that's also a configuration change. So is changing the language of the device. Whatever the new configuration is, as long as you've designed your activity for that configuration, Android takes care of most everything to transition to it, giving the user a seamless experience.

This chapter will take you through the process of a configuration change, from the perspectives of both activities and fragments. We'll show you how to design your application for those transitions and how to avoid traps that could cause your application to crash or misbehave.

The Default Configuration Change Process

The Android operating system keeps track of the current configuration of the device it's running on. Configuration includes lots of factors, and new ones get added all the time. For example, if a device is plugged into a docking station, that represents a change in the device configuration. When a configuration change is detected by Android, callbacks are invoked in running applications to tell them a change is occurring, so an application can properly respond to the change. We'll discuss those callbacks a little later, but for now let's refresh your memory with regard to resources.

One of the great features of Android is that resources get selected for your activity based on the current configuration of the device. You don't need to write code to figure out which configuration is active; you just access resources by name, and Android gets the appropriate resources for you. If the device is in portrait mode and your application requests a layout, you get the portrait layout. If the device is in landscape mode, you get the landscape layout. The code just requests a layout without specifying which one it should get. This is powerful because as new configuration factors get introduced, or new values for configuration factors, the code stays the same. All a developer needs to do is decide if new resources need to be created, and create them as necessary for the new configuration. Then, when the application goes through a configuration change, Android provides the new resources to the application, and everything continues to function as desired.

Because of a great desire to keep things simple, Android destroys the current activity when the configuration changes and creates a new one in its place. This might seem rather harsh, but it's not. It is a bigger challenge to take a running activity and figure out which parts would stay the same and which would not, and then only work with the pieces that need to change.

An activity that's about to be destroyed is properly notified first, giving you a chance to save anything that needs to be saved. When the new activity gets created, it has the opportunity to restore state using data from the previous activity. For a good user experience, obviously you do not want this save and restore to take very long.

It's fairly easy to save any data that you need saved and then let Android throw away the rest and start over, as long as the design of the application and its activities is such that activities don't contain a lot of non-UI stuff that would take a long time to re-create. Therein lies the secret to successful configuration change design: do not put "stuff" inside an activity that cannot be easily re-created during a configuration change.

Keep in mind that our application is not being destroyed, so anything that is in the application context, and not a part of our current activity, will still be there for the new activity. Singletons will still be available, as well as any background threads we might have spun off to do work for our application. Any databases or content providers that we were working with will also still be around. Taking advantage of these makes configuration changes quick and painless. Keep data and business logic outside of activities if you can.

The configuration change process is somewhat similar between activities and fragments. When an activity is being destroyed and re-created, the fragments within that activity get destroyed and re-created. What we need to worry about then is state information about our fragments and activity, such as data currently being displayed to the user, or internal values that we want to preserve. We will save what we want to keep, and pick it up again on the other side when the fragments and activities are being re-created. You'll want to protect data that can't easily be re-created by not letting it get destroyed in the default configuration change process.

The Destroy/Create Cycle of Activities

There are three callbacks to be aware of when dealing with default configuration changes in activities:

- onSaveInstanceState()
- onCreate()
- onRestoreInstanceState()

The first is the callback that Android will invoke when it detects that a configuration change is happening. The activity has a chance to save state that it wants to restore when the new activity gets created at the end of the configuration change. The onSaveInstanceState() callback will be called prior to the call to onStop(). Whatever state exists can be accessed and saved into a Bundle object. This object will get passed in to both of the other callbacks (onCreate() and onRestoreInstanceState()) when the activity is re-created. You only need to put logic in one or the other to restore your activity's state.

The default onSaveInstanceState() callback does some nice things for you. For example, it goes through the currently active view hierarchy and saves the values for each view that has an android:id. This means if you have an EditText view that has received some user input, that input will be available on the other side of the activity destroy/create cycle to populate the EditText before the user gets control back. You do not need to go through and save this state yourself. If you do override onSaveInstanceState(), be sure to call super.onSaveInstanceState() with the bundle object so it can take care of this for you. It's not the views that are saved, only the attributes of their state that should persist across the destroy/create boundary.

To save data in the bundle object, use methods such as putInt() for integers and putString() for strings. There are quite a few methods in the android.os.Bundle class; you are not limited to integers and strings. For example, putParcelable() can be used to save complex objects. Each put is used with a string key, and you will retrieve the value later using the same key used to put the value in. A sample onSaveInstanceState() might look like Listing 2-1.

Listing 2-1. Sample on SaveInstanceState()

```
@Override
public void onSaveInstanceState(Bundle icicle) {
    super.onSaveInstanceState(icicle);
    icicle.putInt("counter", 1);
}
```

Sometimes the bundle is called icicle because it represents a small frozen piece of an activity. In this sample, you only save one value, and it has a key of counter. You could save more values by simply adding more put statements to this callback. The counter value in this example is somewhat temporary because if the application is completely destroyed, the current value will be lost. This could happen if the user turned off their device, for example. In Chapter 4, you'll learn about ways to save values more permanently. This instance state is only meant to hang onto values while the application is running this time. Do not use this mechanism for state that is important to keep for a longer term.

To restore activity state, you access the bundle object to retrieve values that you believe are there. Again, you use methods of the Bundle class such as getInt() and getString() with the appropriate key passed to tell which value you want back. If the key does not exist in the Bundle, a value of 0 or null is passed back (depending on the type of the object being requested). Or you can provide a default value in the appropriate getter method. Listing 2-2 shows a sample onRestoreInstanceState() callback.

Listing 2-2. Sample on RestoreInstanceState()

```
@Override
public void onRestoreInstanceState(Bundle icicle) {
    super.onRestoreInstanceState(icicle);
    int someInt = icicle.getInt("counter", -1);
    // Now go do something with someInt to restore the
    // state of the activity. -1 is the default if no
    // value was found.
}
```

It's up to you whether you restore state in onCreate() or in onRestoreInstanceState(). Many applications will restore state in onCreate() because that is where a lot of initialization is done. One reason to separate the two would be if you're creating an activity class that could be extended. The developers doing the extending might find it easier to just override onRestoreInstanceState() with the code to restore state, as compared to having to override all of onCreate().

What's very important to note here is that you need to be very concerned with references to activities and views and other objects that need to be garbage-collected when the current activity is fully destroyed. If you put something into the saved bundle that refers back to the activity being destroyed, that activity can't be garbage collected. This is very likely a memory leak that could grow and grow until your application crashes. Objects to avoid in bundles include Drawables, Adapters, Views, and anything else that is tied to the activity context. Instead of putting a Drawable into the bundle, serialize the bitmap and save that. Or better yet, manage the bitmaps outside of the activity and fragment instead of inside. Add some sort of reference to the bitmap to the bundle. When it comes time to re-create any Drawables for the new fragment, use the reference to access the outside bitmaps to regenerate your Drawables.

The Destroy/Create Cycle of Fragments

The destroy/create cycle for fragments is very similar to that of activities. A fragment in the process of being destroyed and re-created will have its onSaveInstanceState() callback called, allowing the fragment to save values in a Bundle object for later. One difference is that six fragment callbacks receive this Bundle object when a fragment is being re-created: onInflate(), onCreate(), onCreateView(), onActivityCreated(), onViewCreated(), and onViewStateRestored(). The last two callbacks are more recent, from Honeycomb 3.2 and JellyBean 4.2 respectively. This gives us lots of opportunities to rebuild the internal state of our reconstructed fragment from its previous state.

Android guarantees only that onSaveInstanceState() will be called for a fragment sometime before onDestroy(). That means the view hierarchy may or may not be attached when onSaveInstanceState() is called. Therefore, don't count on traversing the view hierarchy inside of onSaveInstanceState(). For example, if the fragment is on the fragment back stack, no UI will be showing, so no view hierarchy will exist. This is OK of course because if no UI is showing, there is no need to attempt to capture the current values of views to save them. You need to check if a view exists before trying to save its current value, and not consider it an error if the view does not exist.

Just like with activities, be careful not to include items in the bundle object that refer to an activity or to a fragment that might not exist later when this fragment is being re-created. Keep the size of the bundle as small as possible, and as much as possible store long-lasting data outside of activities and fragments and simply refer to it from your activities and fragments. Then your destroy/create cycles will go that much faster, you'll be much less likely to create a memory leak, and your activity and fragment code should be easier to maintain.

Using FragmentManager to Save Fragment State

Fragments have another way to save state, in addition to, or instead of, Android notifying the fragments that their state should be saved. With Honeycomb 3.2, the FragmentManager class got a saveFragmentInstanceState() method that can be called to generate an object of the class Fragment.SavedState. The methods mentioned in the previous sections for saving state do so within the internals of Android. While we know that the state is being saved, we do not have any direct access to it. This method of saving state gives you an object that represents the saved state of a fragment and allows you to control if and when a fragment is created from that state.

The way to use a Fragment.SavedState object to restore a fragment is through the setInitialSavedState() method of the Fragment class. In Chapter 1, you learned that it is best to create new fragments using a static factory method (for example, newInstance()). Within this method, you saw how a default constructor is called and then an arguments bundle is attached. You could instead call the setInitialSavedState() method to set it up for restoration to a previous state.

There are a few caveats you should know about this method of saving fragment state:

- The fragment to be saved must currently be attached to the fragment manager.

- A new fragment created using this saved state must be the same class type as the fragment it was created from.

- The saved state cannot contain dependencies on other fragments. Other fragments may not exist when the saved fragment is re-created.

Using setRetainInstance on a Fragment

A fragment can avoid being destroyed and re-created on a configuration change. If the setRetainInstance() method is called with an argument of true, the fragment will be retained in the application when its activity is being destroyed and re-created. The fragment's onDestroy() callback will not be called, nor will onCreate(). The onDetach() callback will be called because the fragment must be detached from the activity that's going away, and onAttach() and onActivityCreated() will be called because the fragment is attached to a new activity. This only works for fragments that are not on the back stack. It is especially useful for fragments that do not have a UI.

This feature is very powerful in that you can use a non-UI fragment to handle references to your data objects and background threads, and call setRetainInstance(true) on this fragment so it won't get destroyed and re-created on a configuration change. The added bonus is that during the normal configuration change process, the non-UI fragment callbacks onDetach() and onAttach() will switch the activity reference from the old to the new.

Deprecated Configuration Change Methods

A couple of methods on Activity have been deprecated, so you should no longer use them:

- getLastNonConfigurationInstance()
- onRetainNonConfigurationInstance()

These methods previously allowed you to save an arbitrary object from an activity that was being destroyed, to be passed to the next instance of the activity that was being created. Although they were useful, you should now use the methods described earlier instead to manage data between instances of activities in the destroy/create cycle.

Handling Configuration Changes Yourself

So far, you've seen how Android handles configuration changes for you. It takes care of destroying and re-creating activities and fragments, pulling in the best resources for the new configuration, retaining any user-entered data, and giving you the opportunity to execute some extra logic in some callbacks. This is usually going to be your best option. But when it isn't, when you have to handle a configuration change yourself, Android provides a way out. This isn't recommended because it is then completely up to you to determine what needs to change due to the change, and then for you to take care of making all the changes. As mentioned before, there are many configuration changes besides just an orientation change. Luckily, you don't necessarily have to handle all configuration changes yourself.

The first step to handling configuration changes yourself is to declare in the `<activity>` tag in `AndroidManifest.xml` file which changes you're going to handle using the `android:configChanges` attribute. Android will handle the other configuration changes using the previously described methods. You can specify as many configuration change types as needed by or'ing them together with the '|' symbol, like this:

```
<activity  ...   android:configChanges="orientation|keyboardHidden" ... >
```

The complete list of configuration change types can be found on the reference page for R.attr. Be aware that if you target API 13 or higher and you need to handle `orientation`, you also need to handle `screenSize`.

The default process for a configuration change is the invoking of callbacks to destroy and re-create the activity or fragment. When you've declared that you will handle the specific configuration change, the process changes so only the `onConfigurationChanged()` callback is invoked instead, on the activity and its fragments. Android passes in a Configuration object so the callback knows what the new configuration is. It is up to the callback to determine what might have changed; however, since you likely handle only a small number of configuration changes yourself, it shouldn't be too hard to figure this out.

You'd really only want to handle a configuration change yourself when there is very little to be done, when you could skip destroying and re-creating. For example, if the activity layout for portrait and landscape is the same layout and all image resources are the same, destroying and re-creating the activity doesn't really accomplish anything. In this case it would be fairly safe to declare that you will handle the orientation configuration change. During an orientation change of your activity, the activity would remain intact and simply re-render itself in the new orientation using the existing resources such as the layout, images, strings, etc. But it's really not that big a deal to just let Android take care of things if you can.

References

Here are some helpful references to topics you may wish to explore further:

- www.androidbook.com/androidfragments/projects: A list of downloadable projects related to this book. For this chapter, look for a ZIP file called AndroidFragments_Ch02_ConfigChanges.zip. This ZIP file contains all the projects from this chapter, listed in separate root directories. There is also a README.TXT file that describes exactly how to import projects into your IDE from one of these ZIP files.

- http://developer.android.com/guide/topics/fundamentals/activities.html#SavingActivityState: The Android Developer's Guide, which discusses saving and restoring state.

- http://developer.android.com/guide/topics/resources/runtime-changes.html: The Android API Guide for Handling Runtime Changes.

Summary

Let's conclude this chapter by quickly enumerating what you have learned about handling configuration changes:

- Activities by default get destroyed and re-created during configuration changes. So do fragments.

- Avoid putting lots of data and logic into activities so configuration changes occur quickly.

- Let Android provide the appropriate resources.

- Use singletons to hold data outside of activities to make it easier to destroy and re-create activities during configuration changes.

- Take advantage of the default onSaveInstanceState() callback to save UI state on views with android:ids.

- If a fragment can survive with no issues across an activity destroy-and-create cycle, use setRetainInstance() to tell Android it doesn't need to destroy and create the fragment.

Chapter 3

Working with Dialogs

The Android SDK offers extensive support for dialogs. A dialog is a smaller window that pops up in front of the current window to show an urgent message, to prompt the user for a piece of input, or to show some sort of status like the progress of a download. The user is generally expected to interact with the dialog and then return to the window underneath to continue with the application. Technically, Android allows a dialog fragment to also be embedded within an activity's layout, and we'll cover that as well.

Dialogs that are explicitly supported in Android include the alert, prompt, pick-list, single-choice, multiple-choice, progress, time-picker, and date-picker dialogs. (This list could vary depending on the Android release.) Android also supports custom dialogs for other needs. The primary purpose of this chapter is not to cover every single one of these dialogs but to cover the underlying architecture of Android dialogs with a sample application. From there you should be able to use any of the Android dialogs.

It's important to note that Android 3.0 added dialogs based on fragments. The expectation from Google is that developers will only use fragment dialogs, even in the versions of Android before 3.0. This can be done with the fragment-compatibility library. For this reason, this chapter focuses on `DialogFragment`.

Using Dialogs in Android

Dialogs in Android are asynchronous, which provides flexibility. However, if you are accustomed to a programming framework where dialogs are primarily synchronous (such as Microsoft Windows, or JavaScript dialogs in web pages), you might find asynchronous dialogs a bit unintuitive.

With a synchronous dialog, the line of code after the dialog is shown does not run until the dialog has been dismissed. This means the next line of code could interrogate which button was pressed, or what text was typed into the dialog. In Android however, dialogs are asynchronous. As soon as the dialog has been shown, the next line of code runs, even though the user hasn't touched the dialog yet. Your application has to deal with this fact by implementing callbacks from the dialog, to allow the application to be notified of user interaction with the dialog.

This also means your application has the ability to dismiss the dialog from code, which is powerful. If the dialog is displaying a busy message because your application is doing something, as soon as your application has completed that task, it can dismiss the dialog from code.

Understanding Dialog Fragments

In this section, you learn how to use dialog fragments to present a simple alert dialog and a custom dialog that is used to collect prompt text.

DialogFragment Basics

Before we show you working examples of a prompt dialog and an alert dialog, we would like to cover the high-level idea of dialog fragments. Dialog-related functionality uses a class called `DialogFragment`. A `DialogFragment` is derived from the class `Fragment` and behaves much like a fragment. You will then use the `DialogFragment` as the base class for your dialogs. Once you have a derived dialog from this class such as

```
public class MyDialogFragment extends DialogFragment { ... }
```

you can then show this dialog fragment `MyDialogFragment` as a dialog using a fragment transaction. Listing 3-1 shows a code snippet to do this.

Listing 3-1. Showing a Dialog Fragment

```
public class SomeActivity extends Activity
{
    //....other activity functions
    public void showDialog()
    {
        //construct MyDialogFragment
        MyDialogFragment mdf = MyDialogFragment.newInstance(arg1,arg2);
        FragmentManager fm = getFragmentManager();
```

```
        FragmentTransaction ft = fm.beginTransaction();
        mdf.show(ft,"my-dialog-tag");
    }
    //....other activity functions
}
```

> **Note**   We provide a link to a downloadable project at the end of this chapter in the "References" section. You can use this download to experiment with the code and the concepts presented in this chapter.

From Listing 3-1, the steps to show a dialog fragment are as follows:

1. Create a dialog fragment.

2. Get a fragment transaction.

3. Show the dialog using the fragment transaction from step 2.

Let's talk about each of these steps.

Constructing a Dialog Fragment

When constructing a dialog fragment, the rules are the same as when building any other kind of fragment. The recommended pattern is to use a factory method such as newInstance() as you did before. Inside that newInstance() method, you use the default constructor for your dialog fragment, and then you add an arguments bundle that contains your passed-in parameters. You don't want to do other work inside this method because you must make sure that what you do here is the same as what Android does when it restores your dialog fragment from a saved state. And all that Android does is to call the default constructor and re-create the arguments bundle on it.

Overriding onCreateView

When you inherit from a dialog fragment, you need to override one of two methods to provide the view hierarchy for your dialog. The first option is to override onCreateView() and return a view. The second option is to override onCreateDialog() and return a dialog (like the one constructed by an AlertDialog.Builder, which we'll get to shortly).

Listing 3-2 shows an example of overriding the onCreateView().

Listing 3-2. Overriding onCreateView() of a DialogFragment

```
public class MyDialogFragment extends DialogFragment
    implements View.OnClickListener
{
    .....other functions
    public View onCreateView(LayoutInflater inflater,
            ViewGroup container, Bundle savedInstanceState)
    {
        //Create a view by inflating desired layout
        View v =
            inflater.inflate(R.layout.prompt_dialog, container, false);

        //you can locate a view and set values
        TextView tv = (TextView)v.findViewById(R.id.promptmessage);
        tv.setText(this.getPrompt());

        //You can set callbacks on buttons
        Button dismissBtn = (Button)v.findViewById(R.id.btn_dismiss);
        dismissBtn.setOnClickListener(this);

        Button saveBtn = (Button)v.findViewById(R.id.btn_save);
        saveBtn.setOnClickListener(this);
        return v;
    }
    .....other functions
}
```

In Listing 3-2, you are loading a view identified by a layout. Then you look for two buttons and set up callbacks on them. This is very similar to how you created the details fragment in Chapter 1. However, unlike the earlier fragments, a dialog fragment has another way to create the view hierarchy.

Overriding onCreateDialog

As an alternate to supplying a view in onCreateView(), you can override onCreateDialog() and supply a dialog instance. Listing 3-3 supplies sample code for this approach.

Listing 3-3. Overriding onCreateDialog() of a DialogFragment

```
public class MyDialogFragment extends DialogFragment
    implements DialogInterface.OnClickListener
{
    .....other functions
    @Override
    public Dialog onCreateDialog(Bundle icicle)
    {
        AlertDialog.Builder b = new AlertDialog.Builder(getActivity())
            .setTitle("My Dialog Title")
            .setPositiveButton("Ok", this)
            .setNegativeButton("Cancel", this)
            .setMessage(this.getMessage());
        return b.create();
    }
    .....other functions
}
```

In this example, you use the alert dialog builder to create a dialog object to return. This works well for simple dialogs. The first option of overriding onCreateView() is equally easy and provides much more flexibility.

AlertDialog.Builder is actually a carryover from pre-3.0 Android. This is one of the old ways to create a dialog, and it's still available to you to create dialogs within DialogFragments. As you can see, it's fairly easy to build a dialog by calling the various methods available, as we've done here.

Displaying a Dialog Fragment

Once you have a dialog fragment constructed, you need a fragment transaction to show it. Like all other fragments, operations on dialog fragments are conducted through fragment transactions.

The show() method on a dialog fragment takes a fragment transaction as an input. You can see this in Listing 3-1. The show() method uses the fragment transaction to add this dialog to the activity and then commits the fragment transaction. However, the show() method does not add the transaction to the back stack. If you want to do this, you need to add this transaction to the back stack first and then pass it to the show() method. The show() method of a dialog fragment has the following signatures:

```
public int show(FragmentTransaction transaction, String tag)
public int show(FragmentManager manager, String tag)
```

The first show() method displays the dialog by adding this fragment to the passed-in transaction with the specified tag. This method then returns the identifier of the committed transaction.

The second show() method automates getting a transaction from the transaction manager. This is a shortcut method. However, when you use this second method, you don't have an option to add the transaction to the back stack. If you want that control, you need to use the first method. The second method could be used if you wanted to simply display the dialog, and you had no other reason to work with a fragment transaction at that time.

A nice thing about a dialog being a fragment is that the underlying fragment manager does the basic state management. For example, even if the device rotates when a dialog is being displayed, the dialog is reproduced without you performing any state management.

The dialog fragment also offers methods to control the frame in which the dialog's view is displayed, such as the title and the appearance of the frame. Refer to the DialogFragment class documentation to see more of these options; this URL is provided at the end of this chapter.

Dismissing a Dialog Fragment

There are two ways you can dismiss a dialog fragment. The first is to explicitly call the dismiss() method on the dialog fragment in response to a button or some action on the dialog view, as shown in Listing 3-4.

Listing 3-4. Calling dismiss()

```
if (someview.getId() == R.id.btn_dismiss)
{
    //use some callbacks to advise clients
    //of this dialog that it is being dismissed
    //and call dismiss
    dismiss();
    return;
}
```

The dialog fragment's dismiss() method removes the fragment from the fragment manager and then commits that transaction. If there is a back stack for this dialog fragment, then the dismiss() pops the current dialog out of the transaction stack and presents the previous fragment transaction state. Whether there is a back stack or not, calling dismiss() results in calling the standard dialog fragment destroy callbacks, including onDismiss().

One thing to note is that you can't rely on onDismiss() to conclude that a dismiss() has been called by your code. This is because onDismiss() is also called when a device configuration changes and hence is not a good indicator of what the user did to the dialog itself. If the dialog is being displayed when the user rotates the device, the dialog fragment sees onDismiss() called even though the user did not press a button in the dialog. Instead, you should always rely on explicit button clicks on the dialog view.

If the user presses the Back button while the dialog fragment is displayed, this causes the onCancel() callback to fire on the dialog fragment. By default, Android makes the dialog fragment go away, so you don't need to call dismiss() on the fragment yourself. But if you want the calling activity to be notified that the dialog has been cancelled, you need to invoke logic from within onCancel() to make that happen. This is a difference between onCancel() and onDismiss() with dialog fragments. With onDismiss(), you can't be sure exactly what happened that caused the onDismiss() callback to fire. You might also have noticed that a dialog fragment does not have a cancel() method, just dismiss(); but as we said, when a dialog fragment is being cancelled by pressing the Back button, Android takes care of cancelling/dismissing it for you.

The other way to dismiss a dialog fragment is to present another dialog fragment. The way you dismiss the current dialog and present the new one is slightly different than just dismissing the current dialog. Listing 3-5 shows an example.

Listing 3-5. Setting Up a Dialog for a Back Stack

```
if (someview.getId() == R.id.btn_invoke_another_dialog)
{
    Activity act = getActivity();
    FragmentManager fm = act.getFragmentManager();
    FragmentTransaction ft = fm.beginTransaction();
    ft.remove(this);

    ft.addToBackStack(null);
    //null represents no name for the back stack transaction

    HelpDialogFragment hdf =
        HelpDialogFragment.newInstance(R.string.helptext);
    hdf.show(ft, "HELP");
    return;
}
```

Within a single transaction, you're removing the current dialog fragment and adding the new dialog fragment. This has the effect of making the current dialog disappear visually and making the new dialog appear. If the user presses the Back button, because you've saved this transaction on the back stack, the new dialog is dismissed and the previous dialog is displayed. This is a handy way of displaying a help dialog, for example.

Implications of a Dialog Dismiss

When you add any fragment to a fragment manager, the fragment manager does the state management for that fragment. This means when a device configuration changes (for example, the device rotates), the activity is restarted and the fragments are also restarted. You saw this earlier when you rotated the device while running the Shakespeare sample application in chapter 1.

A device-configuration change doesn't affect dialogs because they are also managed by the fragment manager. But the implicit behavior of show() and dismiss() means you can easily lose track of a dialog fragment if you're not careful. The show() method automatically adds the fragment to the fragment manager; the dismiss() method automatically removes the fragment from the fragment manager. You may have a direct pointer to a dialog fragment before you start showing the fragment. But you can't add this fragment to the fragment manager and later call show(), because a fragment can only be added once to the fragment manager. You may plan to retrieve this pointer through restore of the activity. However, if you show and dismiss this dialog, this fragment is implicitly removed from the fragment manager, thereby denying that fragment's ability to be restored and repointed (because the fragment manager doesn't know this fragment exists after it is removed).

If you want to keep the state of a dialog after it is dismissed, you need to maintain the state outside of the dialog either in the parent activity or in a non-dialog fragment that hangs around for a longer time.

DialogFragment Sample Application

In this section, you review a sample application that demonstrates these concepts of a dialog fragment. You also examine communication between a fragment and the activity that contains it. To make it all happen, you need five Java files:

- MainActivity.java: The main activity of your application. It displays a simple view with help text in it and a menu from which dialogs can be started.

- PromptDialogFragment.java: An example of a dialog fragment that defines its own layout in XML and allows input from the user. It has three buttons: Save, Dismiss (cancel), and Help.

- AlertDialogFragment.java: An example of a dialog fragment that uses the AlertBuilder class to create a dialog within this fragment. This is the old-school way of creating a dialog.

- `HelpDialogFragment.java`: A very simple fragment that displays a help message from the application's resources. The specific help message is identified when a help dialog object is created. This help fragment can be shown from both the main activity and the prompt dialog fragment.

- `OnDialogDoneListener.java`: An interface that you require your activity to implement in order to get messages back from the fragments. Using an interface means your fragments don't need to know much about the calling activity, except that it must have implemented this interface. This helps encapsulate functionality where it belongs. From the activity's point of view, it has a common way to receive information back from fragments without needing to know too much about them.

There are three layouts for this application: for the main activity, for the prompt dialog fragment, and for the help dialog fragment. Note that you don't need a layout for the alert dialog fragment because the `AlertBuilder` takes care of that layout for you internally. When you're done, the application looks like Figure 3-1.

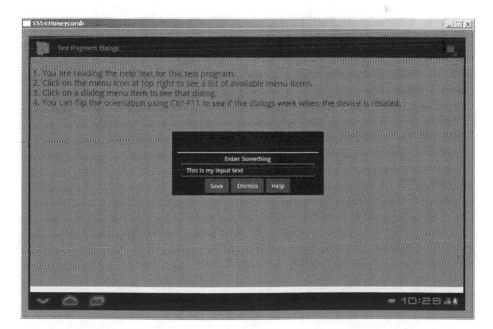

Figure 3-1. The user interface for the dialog fragment sample application

Dialog Sample: MainActivity

Let's get to the source code, which you can download from the book's web site (see the "References" section). We'll use the DialogFragmentDemo project. Open up the source code for `MainActivity.java` before we continue.

The code for the main activity is very straightforward. You display a simple page of text and set up a menu. Each menu item invokes an activity method, and each method does basically the same thing: gets a fragment transaction, creates a new fragment, and shows the fragment. Note that each fragment has a unique tag that's used with the fragment transaction. This tag becomes associated with the fragment in the fragment manager, so you can locate these fragments later by tag name. The fragment can also determine its own tag value with the `getTag()` method on `Fragment`.

The last method definition in the main activity is `onDialogDone()`, which is a callback that is part of the `OnDialogDoneListener` interface that your activity is implementing. As you can see, the callback supplies a tag of the fragment that is calling you, a boolean value indicating whether the dialog fragment was cancelled, and a message. For your purposes, you merely want to log the information to LogCat; you also show it to the user using `Toast`. Toast will be covered later in this chapter.

Dialog Sample: OnDialogDoneListener

So that you can know when a dialog has gone away, create a listener interface that your dialog callers implement. The code of the interface is in OnDialogDoneListener.java.

This is a very simple interface, as you can see. You choose only one callback for this interface, which the activity must implement. Your fragments don't need to know the specifics of the calling activity, only that the calling activity must implement the `OnDialogDoneListener` interface; therefore the fragments can call this callback to communicate with the calling activity. Depending on what the fragment is doing, there could be multiple callbacks in the interface. For this sample application, you're showing the interface separately from the fragment class definitions. For easier management of code, you could embed the fragment listener interface inside of the fragment class definition itself, thus making it easier to keep the listener and the fragment in sync with each other.

Dialog Sample: PromptDialogFragment

Now let's look at your first fragment, `PromptDialogFragment`, whose layout is in /res/layout/prompt_dialog.xml and Java code is under /src in PromptDialogFragment.java.

This prompt dialog layout looks like many you've seen previously. There is a TextView to serve as the prompt; an EditText to take the user's input; and three buttons for saving the input, dismissing (cancelling) the dialog fragment, and popping a help dialog.

The PromptDialogFragment Java code starts out looking just like your earlier fragments. You have a newInstance() static method to create new objects, and within this method you call the default constructor, build an arguments bundle, and attach it to your new object. Next, you have something new in the onAttach() callback. You want to make sure the activity you just got attached to has implemented the OnDialogDoneListener interface. In order to test that, you cast the activity passed in to the OnDialogDoneListener interface. Here's that code:

```
try {
    OnDialogDoneListener test = (OnDialogDoneListener)act;
}
catch(ClassCastException cce) {
    // Here is where we fail gracefully.
    Log.e(MainActivity.LOGTAG, "Activity is not listening");
}
```

If the activity does not implement this interface, a ClassCastException is thrown. You could handle this exception and deal with it more gracefully, but this example keeps the code as simple as possible.

Next up is the onCreate() callback. As is common with fragments, you don't build your user interface here, but you can set the dialog style. This is unique to dialog fragments. You can set both the style and the theme yourself, or you can set just style and use a theme value of zero (0) to let the system choose an appropriate theme for you. Here's that code:

```
int style = DialogFragment.STYLE_NORMAL, theme = 0;
setStyle(style,theme);
```

In onCreateView() you create the view hierarchy for your dialog fragment. Just like other fragments, you do not attach your view hierarchy to the view container passed in (that is, by setting the attachToRoot parameter to false). You then proceed to set up the button callbacks, and you set the dialog prompt text to the prompt that was passed originally to newInstance(). Finally, you check to see whether any values are being passed in through the saved state bundle (icicle). This would indicate that your fragment is being re-created, most likely due to a configuration change, and it's possible that the user has already typed some text. If so, you need to populate the EditText with what the user has done so far. Remember that because your configuration has changed, the actual view object in memory is not the same as before, so you must locate it and set the text accordingly. The very next callback is onSaveInstanceState(); it's where you save any current text typed by the user into the saved state bundle.

The onCancel() and onDismiss() callbacks are not shown because all they do is logging; you'll be able to see when these callbacks fire during the fragment's lifecycle.

The final callback in the prompt dialog fragment is for the buttons. Once again, you grab a reference to your enclosing activity and cast it to the interface you expect the activity to have implemented. If the user pressed the Save button, you grab the text as entered and call the interface's callback onDialogDone(). This callback takes the tag name of this fragment, a boolean indicating whether this dialog fragment was cancelled, and a message, which in this case is the text typed by the user. Here it is from the MainActivity:

```
public void onDialogDone(String tag, boolean cancelled,
                         CharSequence message) {
    String s = tag + " responds with: " + message;
    if(cancelled)
        s = tag + " was cancelled by the user";
    Toast.makeText(this, s, Toast.LENGTH_LONG).show();
    Log.v(LOGTAG, s);
}
```

To finish handling a click on the Save button, you then call dismiss() to get rid of the dialog fragment. Remember that dismiss() not only makes the fragment go away visually, but also pops the fragment out of the fragment manager so it is no longer available to you.

If the button pressed is Dismiss, you again call the interface callback, this time with no message, and then you call dismiss(). And finally, if the user pressed the Help button, you don't want to lose the prompt dialog fragment, so you do something a little different. We described this earlier. In order to remember the prompt dialog fragment so you can come back to it later, you need to create a fragment transaction to remove the prompt dialog fragment and add the help dialog fragment with the show() method; this needs to go onto the back stack. Notice, too, how the help dialog fragment is created with a reference to a resource ID. This means your help dialog fragment can be used with any help text available to your application.

Dialog Sample: HelpDialogFragment

You created a fragment transaction to go from the prompt dialog fragment to the help dialog fragment, and you placed that fragment transaction on the back stack. This has the effect of making the prompt dialog fragment disappear from view, but it's still accessible through the fragment manager and the back stack. The new help dialog fragment appears in its place and allows the user to read the help text. When the user dismisses the help dialog fragment, the fragment back stack entry is popped, with the effect of the help dialog fragment being dismissed (both visually and from the fragment manager) and the prompt dialog fragment restored to view. This is a pretty easy way to make all this happen. It is very simple yet very powerful; it even works if the user rotates the device while these dialogs are being displayed.

Look at the source code of the HelpDialogFragment.java file and its layout (help_dialog.xml). The point of this dialog fragment is to display help text. The layout is a TextView and a Close button. The Java code should be starting to look familiar to you. There's a newInstance() method to create a new help dialog fragment, an onCreate() method to set the style and theme, and an onCreateView() method to build the view hierarchy. In this particular case, you want to locate a string resource to populate the TextView, so you access the resources through the activity and choose the resource ID that was passed in to newInstance(). Finally, onCreateView() sets up a button-click handler to capture the clicks of the Close button. In this case, you don't need to do anything interesting at the time of dismissal.

This fragment is called two ways: from the activity and from the prompt dialog fragment. When this help dialog fragment is shown from the main activity, dismissing it simply pops the fragment off the top and reveals the main activity underneath. When this help dialog fragment is shown from the prompt dialog fragment, because the help dialog fragment was part of a fragment transaction on the back stack, dismissing it causes the fragment transaction to be rolled back, which pops the help dialog fragment but restores the prompt dialog fragment. The user sees the prompt dialog fragment reappear.

Dialog Sample: AlertDialogFragment

We have one last dialog fragment to show you in this sample application: the alert dialog fragment. Although you could create an alert dialog fragment in a way similar to the help dialog fragment, you can also create a dialog fragment using the old AlertBuilder framework that has worked for many releases of Android. Look at the source code in AlertDialogFragment.java.

You don't need a layout for this one because the AlertBuilder takes care of that for you. Note that this dialog fragment starts out like any other, but instead of an onCreateView() callback, you have a onCreateDialog() callback. You implement either onCreateView() or onCreateDialog() but not both. The return from onCreateDialog() is not a view; it's a dialog. Of interest here is that to get parameters for the dialog, you should be accessing your arguments bundle. In this example application, you only do this for the alert message, but you could access other parameters through the arguments bundle as well.

Notice also that with this type of dialog fragment, you need your fragment class to implement the DialogInterface.OnClickListener, which means your dialog fragment must implement the onClick() callback. This callback is fired when the user acts on the embedded dialog. Once again, you get a reference to the dialog that fired and an indication of which button was pressed. As before, you should be careful not to depend on an onDismiss() because this could fire when there is a device configuration change.

Dialog Sample: Embedded Dialogs

There's one more feature of a DialogFragment that you may have noticed. In the main layout for the application, under the text, is a FrameLayout that can be used to hold a dialog. In the application's menu, the last item causes a fragment transaction to add a new instance of a PromptDialogFragment to the main screen. Without any modifications, the dialog fragment can be displayed embedded in the main layout, and it functions as you would expect.

One thing that is different about this technique is that the code to show the embedded dialog is not the same as the code to do a pop-up dialog. The embedded dialog code looks like this:

```
ft.add(R.id.embeddedDialog, pdf, EMBED_DIALOG_TAG);
ft.commit();
```

This looks just the same as in Chapter 1, when we displayed a fragment in a FrameLayout. This time, however, you make sure to pass in a tag name, which is used when the dialog fragment notifies your activity of the user's input.

Dialog Sample: Observations

When you run this sample application, make sure you try all the menu options in different orientations of the device. Rotate the device while the dialog fragments are displayed. You should be pleased to see that the dialogs go with the rotations; you do not need to worry about a lot of code to manage the saving and restoring of fragments due to configuration changes.

The other thing we hope you appreciate is the ease with which you can communicate between the fragments and the activity. Of course, the activity has references, or can get references, to all the available fragments, so it can access methods exposed by the fragments themselves. This isn't the only way to communicate between fragments and the activity. You can always use the getter methods on the fragment manager to retrieve an instance of a managed fragment, and then cast that reference appropriately and call a method on that fragment directly. You can even do this from within another fragment. The degree to which you isolate your fragments from each other with interfaces and through activities, or build in dependencies with fragment-to-fragment communication, is based on how complex your application is and how much reuse you want to achieve.

Working with Toast

A Toast is like a mini alert dialog that has a message and displays for a certain amount of time and then goes away automatically. It does not have any buttons. So it can be said that it is a transient alert message. It's called Toast because it pops up like toast out of a toaster.

Listing 3-6 shows an example of how you can show a message using Toast.

Listing 3-6. Using Toast for Debugging

```
//Create a function to wrap a message as a toast
//show the toast
public void reportToast(String message)
{
    String s = MainActivity.LOGTAG + ":" + message;
    Toast.makeText(activity, s, Toast.LENGTH_SHORT).show();
}
```

The makeText() method in Listing 3-6 can take not only an activity but any context object, such as the one passed to a broadcast receiver or a service, for example. This extends the use of Toast outside of activities.

References

▓ www.androidbook.com/androidfragments/projects:
   This chapter's test project. The name of the ZIP file is
   AndroidFragments_ch03_Dialogs.zip. The download
   includes an example of the date- and time-picker
   dialogs in PickerDialogFragmentDemo.

▓ http://developer.android.com/guide/topics/ui/
   dialogs.html: Android SDK document that provides an
   excellent introduction to working with Android dialogs.
   You will find here an explanation of how to use managed
   dialogs and various examples of available dialogs.

- http://developer.android.com/reference/android/
  content/DialogInterface.html: The many constants
  defined for dialogs.

- http://developer.android.com/reference/android/
  app/AlertDialog.Builder.html: API documentation for
  the AlertDialog builder class.

- http://developer.android.com/reference/android/
  app/ProgressDialog.html: API documentation for
  ProgressDialog.

- http://developer.android.com/guide/topics/ui/
  controls/pickers.html: An Android tutorial for using
  the date-picker and time-picker dialogs.

Summary

This chapter discussed asynchronous dialogs and how to use dialog
fragments, including the following topics:

- What a dialog is and why you use one

- The asynchronous nature of a dialog in Android

- The three steps of getting a dialog to display
  on the screen

- Creating a fragment

- Two methods for how a dialog fragment can create
  a view hierarchy

- How a fragment transaction is involved in displaying
  a dialog fragment, and how to get one

- What happens when the user presses the Back button
  while viewing a dialog fragment

- The back stack, and managing dialog fragments

- What happens when a button on a dialog fragment is
  clicked, and how you deal with it

- A clean way to communicate back to the calling activity
  from a dialog fragment

- How one dialog fragment can call another dialog fragment
  and still get back to the previous dialog fragment

- The Toast class and how it can be used as a simple
  alert pop-up

Chapter 4

Working with Preferences and Saving State

Android offers a robust and flexible framework for dealing with settings, also known as preferences. And by settings, we mean those feature choices that a user makes and saves to customize an application to their liking. (In this chapter, the terms settings and preferences will be used interchangeably.) For example, if the user wants a notification via a ringtone or vibration or not at all, that is a preference the user saves; the application remembers the choice until the user changes it. Android provides simple APIs that hide the management and persisting of preferences. It also provides prebuilt user interfaces that you can use to let the user make preference selections. Because of the power built into the Android preferences framework, we can also use preferences for more general-purpose storing of application state, to allow our application to pick up where it left off, should our application go away and come back later. As another example, a game's high scores could be stored as preferences, although you'll want to use your own UI to display them.

This chapter covers how to implement your own settings screens for your application, how to interact with Android system settings, and how to use settings to secretly save application state, and it also provides best-practice guidance. You'll discover how to make your settings look good on small screens as well as larger screens such as those found on tablets.

Exploring the Preferences Framework

Android's preferences framework builds from the individual settings choices, to a hierarchy of screens that contain settings choices. Settings could be binary settings such as on/off, or text input, or a numeric value, or could be a selection from a list of choices. Android uses a `PreferenceManager` to provide settings values to applications. The framework takes care of making and persisting changes, and notifying the application when a setting changes or is about to change. While settings are persisted in files, applications don't deal directly with the files. The files are hidden away, and you'll see shortly where they are.

Preferences can be specified with XML, or by writing code. For this chapter, you'll work with a sample application that demonstrates the different types of choices. XML is the preferred way to specify a preference, so that is how the application was written. XML specifies the lowest-level settings, plus how to group settings together into categories and screens. For reference, the sample application for this chapter presents the following settings as shown in Figure 4-1.

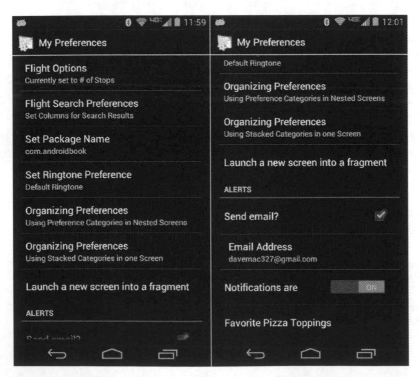

Figure 4-1. The main settings from the sample app preference UI. Due to the screen's height, it has been shown with the top on the left and the bottom on the right. Notice the overlap between the two images

Android provides an end-to-end preferences framework. This means the framework lets you define your preferences, display the setting(s) to the user, and persist the user's selection to the data store. You define your preferences in XML under /res/xml/. To show preferences to the user, you write an activity class that extends a predefined Android class called android.preference.PreferenceActivity and use fragments to handle the screens of preferences. The framework takes care of the rest (displaying and persisting). Within your application, your code will get references to specific preferences. With a preference reference, you can get the current value of the preference.

In order for preferences to be saved across user sessions, the current values must be saved somewhere. The Android framework takes care of persisting preferences in an XML file within the application's /data/data directory on the device (see Figure 4-2).

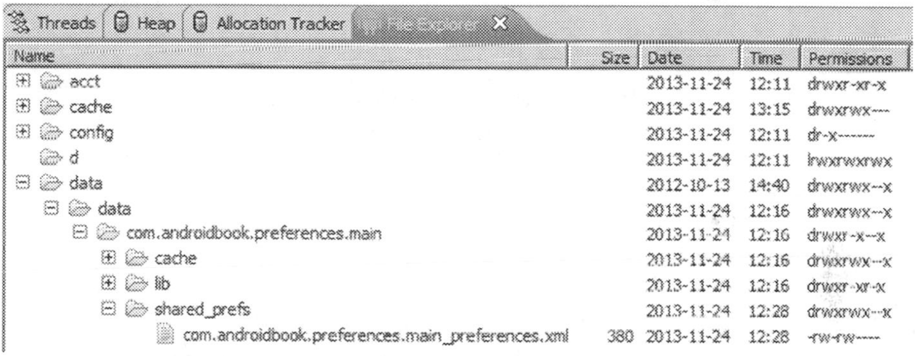

Name		Size	Date	Time	Permissions
⊞ 📂 acct			2013-11-24	12:11	drwxr-xr-x
⊞ 📂 cache			2013-11-24	13:15	drwxrwx---
⊞ 📂 config			2013-11-24	12:11	dr-x------
📂 d			2013-11-24	12:11	lrwxrwxrwx
⊟ 📂 data			2012-10-13	14:40	drwxrwx--x
⊟ 📂 data			2013-11-24	12:16	drwxrwx--x
⊟ 📂 com.androidbook.preferences.main			2013-11-24	12:16	drwxr-x--x
⊞ 📂 cache			2013-11-24	12:16	drwxrwx--x
⊞ 📂 lib			2013-11-24	12:16	drwxr-xr-x
⊟ 📂 shared_prefs			2013-11-24	12:28	drwxrwx--x
📄 com.androidbook.preferences.main_preferences.xml		380	2013-11-24	12:28	-rw-rw----

Figure 4-2. Path to an application's saved preferences

> **Note** You will be able to inspect shared preferences files in the emulator only. On a real device, the shared preferences files are not readable due to Android security (unless you have root privileges, of course).

The default preferences file path for an application is /data/data/[PACKAGE_NAME]/shared_prefs/[PACKAGE_NAME]_preferences.xml, where [PACKAGE_NAME] is the package of the application. Listing 4-1 shows the com.androidbook.preferences.main_preferences.xml data file for this example.

Listing 4-1. Saved Preferences for Our Example

```
<?xml version='1.0' encoding='utf-8' standalone='yes' ?>
<map>
<boolean name="notification_switch" value="true" />
<string name="package_name_preference">com.androidbook.win</string>
<boolean name="potato_selection_pref" value="true" />
<boolean name="show_airline_column_pref" value="true" />
<string name="flight_sort_option">2</string>
<boolean name="alert_email" value="false" />
<set name="pizza_toppings">
<string>pepperoni</string>
<string>cheese</string>
<string>olive</string>
</set>
<string name="alert_email_address">davemac327@gmail.com</string>
</map>
```

As you can see, values are stored in a map, with preference keys as names to the data values. Some of the values look cryptic and do not match what is displayed to the user. For example, the value for flight_sort_option is 2. Android does not store the displayed text as the value of the preference; rather, it stores a value that the user won't see, that you can use independently of what the user sees. You want the freedom to change the displayed text based on the user's language, and you also want the ability to tweak the displayed text while keeping the same stored value in the preferences file. You might even be able to do simpler processing of the preference if the value is an integer instead of some display string. What you don't have to worry about is parsing this data file. The Android preferences framework provides a nice API for dealing with preferences, which will be described in more detail later in this chapter.

If you compare the preferences map in Listing 4-1 with the screenshots in Figure 4-1, you will notice that not all preferences are listed with values in the preferences XML data file. This is because the preference data file does not automatically store a default value for you. You'll see shortly how to deal with default values.

Now that you've seen where the values are saved, you need to see how to define the screens to display to the user so they can make selections. Before you see how to collect preferences together into screens, you'll learn about the different types of preferences you can use, and then you'll see how to put them together into screens. Each persisted value in the /data/ data XML file is from a specific preference. So let's understand what each of these means.

Understanding CheckBoxPreference and SwitchPreference

The simplest of the preferences are the `CheckBoxPreference` and `SwitchPreference`. These share a common parent class (`TwoStatePreference`) and are either on (value is true) or off (value is false). For the sample application, a screen was created with five `CheckBoxPreferences`, as shown in Figure 4-3. Listing 4-2 shows what the XML looks like for a `CheckBoxPreference`.

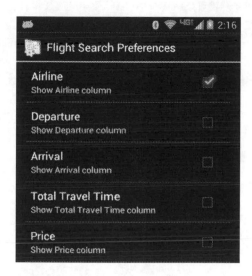

Figure 4-3. The user interface for the check box preference

Listing 4-2. Using CheckBoxPreference

```
<CheckBoxPreference
        android:key="show_airline_column_pref"
        android:title="Airline"
        android:summary="Show Airline column" />
```

> **Note**   We will give you a URL at the end of the chapter that you can use to download projects from this chapter. This will allow you to import these projects into your IDE directly. The main sample application is called PrefDemo. You should refer to that project until you come to the Saving State section.

This example shows the minimum that's required to specify a preference. The key is the reference to, or name of, the preference, the title is the title displayed for the preference, and summary is a description of what the preference is for or a status of the current setting. Looking back on the saved values in Listing 4-1, you will see a <boolean> tag for "show_airline_column_pref" (the key), and it has an attribute value of true, which indicates that the preference is checked on.

With CheckBoxPreference, the state of the preference is saved when the user sets the state. In other words, when the user checks or unchecks the preference control, its state is saved immediately.

The SwitchPreference is very similar except that the visual display is different. Instead of a check box in the user interface, the user sees an on-off switch, as shown in Figure 4-1 next to "Notifications are."

One other useful feature of CheckBoxPreference and SwitchPreference is that you can set different summary text depending on whether it's checked. The XML attributes are summaryOn and summaryOff. If you look in the main. xml file for the CheckBoxPreference called "potato_selection_pref" you will see an example of this.

Before you learn the other preference types, now would be a good time to understand how to access this preference to read its value and perform other operations.

Accessing a Preference Value in Code

Now that you have a preference defined you need to know how to access the preference in code so you can read the value. Listing 4-3 shows code to access the SharedPreferences object in Android where the preferences exist. This code is from the MainActivity.java file in the setOptionText() method.

Listing 4-3. Accessing the CheckBoxPreference

```
    SharedPreferences prefs =
            PreferenceManager.getDefaultSharedPreferences(this);
//  This is the other way to get to the shared preferences:
//  SharedPreferences prefs = getSharedPreferences(
//          "com.androidbook.preferences.main_preferences", 0);
    boolean showAirline = prefs.getBoolean("show_airline_column_pref",
    false);
```

Using the reference to preferences, it is straightforward to read the current value of the show_airline_column_pref preference. As shown in Listing 4-3, there are two ways to get to the preferences. The first way shown is to get the default preferences for the current context. In this case, the context is that of the MainActivity of our application. The second case, which is shown commented out, retrieves the preferences using a package name. You could use whatever package name you want in case you need to store different sets of preferences in different files.

Once you have a reference to the preferences, you call the appropriate getter method with the key of the preference and a default value. Since show_airline_column_pref is a TwoStatePreference, the value returned is a boolean. The default value for show_airline_column_pref is hard-coded here as false. If this preference has not yet been set at all, the hard-coded value (false) will be assigned to showAirline. However, that by itself does not persist the preference to false for future use, nor does it honor any default value that might have been set in the XML specification for this preference. If the XML specification uses a resource value to specify the default value, then the same resource could be referred to in code to set the default value, as shown in the following for a different preference:

```
String flight_option = prefs.getString(
        resources.getString(R.string.flight_sort_option),
        resources.getString(R.string.flight_sort_option_default_value));
```

Notice here that the key for the preference is also using a string resource value (R.string.flight_sort_option). This can be a wise choice since it makes typos less likely. If the resource name is typed wrong you'll very likely get a build error. If you use just simple strings, it is possible for a typo to go unnoticed, except that your preferences won't work.

We showed one way to read a default value for a preference in code. Android provides another way that is a bit more elegant. In onCreate(), you can do the following instead:

```
PreferenceManager.setDefaultValues(this, R.xml.main, false);
```

Then, in setOptionText(), you would have done this to read the option value:

```
String option = prefs.getString(
    resources.getString(R.string.flight_sort_option), null);
```

The first call will use main.xml to find the default values and generate the preferences XML data file for us using the default values. If we already have an instance of the SharedPreferences object in memory, it will update that too. The second call will then find a value for flight_sort_option, because we took care of loading defaults first.

After running this code the first time, if you look in the shared_prefs folder, you will see the preferences XML file even if the preferences screen has not yet been invoked. You will also see another file called _has_set_default_values.xml. This file tells your application that the preferences XML file has already been created with the default values. The third argument to setDefaultValues()—that is, false—indicates that you want the defaults set in the preferences XML file only if it hasn't been done before. Android remembers this information through the existence of this new XML file. However, Android remembers even if you upgrade your application and add new settings with new default values, which means this trick won't set those new defaults. Your best option is to always use a resource for the default value, and always provide that resource as the default value when getting the current value of a preference.

Understanding ListPreference

A list preference contains radio buttons for each option, and the default (or current) selection is preselected. The user is expected to select one and only one of the choices. When the user chooses an option, the dialog is immediately dismissed and the choice is saved in the preferences XML file. Figure 4-4 shows what this looks like.

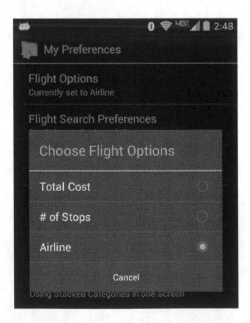

Figure 4-4. The user interface for the ListPreference

Listing 4-4. Specifying a ListPreference in XML

```
<ListPreference
  android:key="@string/flight_sort_option"
  android:title="@string/listTitle"
  android:summary="@string/listSummary"
  android:entries="@array/flight_sort_options"
  android:entryValues="@array/flight_sort_options_values"
  android:dialogTitle="@string/dialogTitle"
  android:defaultValue="@string/flight_sort_option_default_value" />
```

Listing 4-4 contains an XML fragment that represents the flight-option preference setting. This time the file contains references to strings and to arrays, which would be the more common way to specify these rather than hard-coding the strings. As mentioned before, the value of a list preference as stored in the XML data file under the /data/data/{package} directory is not the same as what the user sees in the user interface. The name of the key is stored in the data file, along with a hidden value that the user does not see. Therefore, to get a ListPreference to work, there needs to be two arrays: the values displayed to the user and the strings used as key values. This is where you can easily get tripped up. The entries array holds the strings displayed to the user, and the entryValues array holds the strings that will be stored in the preferences data XML file.

The elements between the two arrays correspond to each other positionally. That is, the third element in the entryValues array corresponds to the third element in the entries array. It is tempting to use 0, 1, 2, etc., as entryValues but it is not required, and it could cause problems later when the arrays must be modified. If our option were numeric in nature (for example, a countdown timer starting value), then we could have used values such as 60, 120, 300, and so on. The values don't need to be numeric at all as long as they make sense to the developer; the user doesn't see these values unless you choose to expose them. The user only sees the text from the first string array flight_sort_options. The example application for this chapter shows it both ways.

A word of caution here: because the preferences XML data file is storing only the value and not the text, should you ever upgrade your application and change the text of the options or add items to the string arrays, any value stored in the preferences XML data file should still line up with the appropriate text after the upgrade. The preferences XML data file is kept during the application upgrade. If the preferences XML data file had a "1" in it, and that meant "# of Stops" before the upgrade, it should still mean "# of Stops" after the upgrade.

Since the entryValues array is not seen by the end user, it is best practice
to store it once and only once within your application. Therefore, make one
and only one /res/values/prefvaluearrays.xml file to contain these arrays.
The entries array is very likely to be created multiple times per application,
for different languages or perhaps different device configurations. Therefore,
make separate prefdisplayarrays.xml files for each variation that you need.
For example, if your application will be used in English and in French, there
will be separate prefdisplayarrays.xml files for English and French. You
do not want to include the entryValues array in each of these other files.
It is imperative though that there are the same numbers of array elements
between entryValues and entries arrays. The elements must line up. When
you make changes, be careful to keep everything in alignment. Listing 4-5
contains the source of ListPreference files for the example.

Listing 4-5. Other ListPreference Files from Our Example

```xml
<?xml version="1.0" encoding="utf-8"?>
<!-- This file is /res/values/prefvaluearrays.xml -->
<resources>
<string-array name="flight_sort_options_values">
    <item>0</item>
    <item>1</item>
    <item>2</item>
</string-array>
<string-array name="pizza_toppings_values">
    <item>cheese</item>
    <item>pepperoni</item>
    <item>onion</item>
    <item>mushroom</item>
    <item>olive</item>
    <item>ham</item>
    <item>pineapple</item>
</string-array>
<string-array name="default_pizza_toppings">
    <item>cheese</item>
    <item>pepperoni</item>
</string-array>
</resources>

<?xml version="1.0" encoding="utf-8"?>
<!-- This file is /res/values/prefdisplayarrays.xml -->
<resources>
<string-array name="flight_sort_options">
    <item>Total Cost</item>
    <item># of Stops</item>
    <item>Airline</item>
</string-array>
<string-array name="pizza_toppings">
```

```
<item>Cheese</item>
<item>Pepperoni</item>
<item>Onions</item>
<item>Portobello Mushrooms</item>
<item>Black Olives</item>
<item>Smoked Ham</item>
<item>Pineapple</item>
</string-array>
</resources>
```

Also, don't forget that your default value as specified in the XML source file must match an entryValue in the array from prefvaluearrays.xml.

For a ListPreference, the value of the preference is a String. If you are using number strings (e.g., 0, 1, 1138) as entryValues, you could convert those to integers or whatever you need in your code, as is used in the flight_sort_options_values array.

Your code is likely going to want to display the user-friendly text from the preference's entries array. This example took a shortcut, because array indices were used for the elements in flight_sort_options_values. By simply converting the value to an int, you know which string to read from flight_sort_options. Had you used some other set of values for flight_sort_options_values, you would need to determine the index of the element that is your preference and then turn around and use that index to grab the text of your preference from flight_sort_options. ListPreference's helper method findIndexOfValue() can help with this, by providing the index into the values array so you can then easily get the corresponding display text from the entries array.

Returning now to Listing 4-4, there are several strings for titles, summaries, and more. The string called flight_sort_option_default_value sets the default value to 1 to represent "# of Stops" in the example. It is usually a good idea to choose a default value for each option. If you don't choose a default value and no value has yet been chosen, the methods that return the value of the option will return null. Your code would have to deal with null values in this case.

Understanding EditTextPreference

The preferences framework also provides a free-form text preference called EditTextPreference. This preference allows you to capture raw text rather than ask the user to make a selection. To demonstrate this, let's assume you have an application that generates Java code for the user. One of the preference settings of this application might be the default package name to use for the generated classes. Here, you want to display a text field to the user for setting the package name for the generated classes. Figure 4-5 shows the UI, and Listing 4-6 shows the XML.

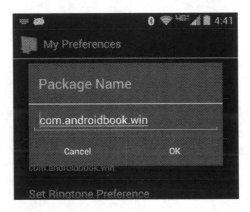

Figure 4-5. *Using the* `EditTextPreference`

Listing 4-6. *An Example of an* `EditTextPreference`

```
<EditTextPreference
        android:key="package_name_preference"
        android:title="Set Package Name"
        android:summary="Set the package name for generated code"
        android:dialogTitle="Package Name" />
```

When Set Package Name is selected, the user is presented with a dialog to input the package name. When the OK button is clicked, the preference is saved to the preference store.

As with the other preferences, you can obtain the value of the preference by calling the appropriate getter method, in this case `getString()`.

Understanding MultiSelectListPreference

And finally, a preference called `MultiSelectListPreference` was introduced in Android 3.0. The concept is somewhat similar to a `ListPreference`, but instead of only being able to select one item in the list, the user can select several or none. In Listing 4-1, the `MultiSelectListPreference` stores a `<set name="pizza_toppings">` tag in the preferences XML data file, instead of a single value. The other significant difference with a `MultiSelectListPreference` is that the default value is an array just like the `entryValues` array. That is, the array for the default values must contain zero or more of the elements from the entryValues array for this preference. This can also be seen in the sample application for this chapter; just view the end of the main.xml file in the /res/xml directory.

To get the current value of a MultiSelectListPreference, use the getStringSet() method of SharedPreferences. To retrieve the display strings from the entries array, you would need to iterate through the set of strings that is the value of this preference, determine the index of the string, and use the index to access the proper display string from the entries array.

Updating AndroidManifest.xml

Because there are two activities in the sample application, we need two activity tags in AndroidManifest.xml. The first one is a standard activity of category LAUNCHER. The second one is for a PreferenceActivity, so set the action name according to convention for intents, and set the category to PREFERENCE as shown in Listing 4-7. You probably don't want the PreferenceActivity showing up on the Android page with all our other applications, which is why you don't use LAUNCHER for it. You would need to make similar changes to AndroidManifest.xml if you were to add other preference activities.

Listing 4-7. PreferenceActivity Entry in AndroidManifest.xml

```
<activity android:name=".MainPreferenceActivity"
        android:label="@string/prefTitle">
    <intent-filter>
        <action android:name=
        "com.androidbook.preferences.main.intent.action.MainPreferences" />
        <category
            android:name="android.intent.category.PREFERENCE" />
    </intent-filter>
</activity>
```

Using PreferenceCategory

The preferences framework provides support for you to organize your preferences into categories. If you have a lot of preferences, for example, you can use PreferenceCategory, which groups preferences under a separator label. Figure 4-6 shows what this could look like. Notice the separators called "MEATS" and "VEGETABLES." You can find the specifications for these in /res/xml/main.xml.

Figure 4-6. Using `PreferenceCategory` to organize preferences

Creating Child Preferences with Dependency

Another way to organize preferences is to use a preference dependency. This creates a parent-child relationship between preferences. For example, you might have a preference that turns on alerts; and if alerts are on, there might be several other alert-related preferences to choose from. If the main alerts preference is off, the other preferences are not relevant and should be disabled. Listing 4-8 shows the XML, and Figure 4-7 shows what it looks like.

Listing 4-8. Preference Dependency in XML

```
<PreferenceScreen>
    <PreferenceCategory
            android:title="Alerts">

        <CheckBoxPreference
                android:key="alert_email"
                android:title="Send email?" />
```

```
<EditTextPreference
        android:key="alert_email_address"
        android:layout="?android:attr/preferenceLayoutChild"
        android:title="Email Address"
        android:dependency="alert_email" />

    </PreferenceCategory>
</PreferenceScreen>
```

Figure 4-7. *Preference dependency*

Preferences with Headers

Android 3.0 introduced a new way to organize preferences. You see this on tablets under the main Settings app. Because tablet screen real estate offers much more room than a smartphone does, it makes sense to display more preference information at the same time. To accomplish this, you use preference headers. Take a look at Figure 4-8.

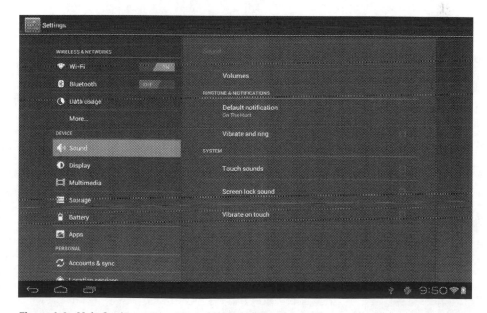

Figure 4-8. *Main Settings page with preference headers*

Notice that headers appear down the left side, like a vertical tab bar. As you click each item on the left, the screen to the right displays the preferences for that item. In Figure 4-8, Sound is chosen, and the sound preferences are displayed at right. The right side is a PreferenceScreen object, and this setup uses fragments. Obviously, we need to do something different than what has been discussed so far in this chapter.

The big change from Android 3.0 was the addition of headers to PreferenceActivity. This also means using a new callback within PreferenceActivity to do the headers setup. Now, when you extend PreferenceActivity, you'll want to implement this method:

```
public void onBuildHeaders(List<Header> target) {
    loadHeadersFromResource(R.xml.preferences, target);
}
```

Please refer to the PrefDemo sample application for the complete source code. The preferences.xml file contains some new tags that look like this:

```
<preference-headers
        xmlns:android="http://schemas.android.com/apk/res/android">
    <header android:fragment="com.example.PrefActivity$Prefs1Fragment"
            android:icon="@drawable/ic_settings_sound"
            android:title="Sound"
            android:summary="Your sound preferences" />
    ...
```

Each header tag points to a class that extends PreferenceFragment. In the example just given, the XML specifies an icon, the title, and summary text (which acts like a subtitle). Prefs1Fragment is an inner class of PreferenceActivity that could look something like this:

```
public static class Prefs1Fragment extends PreferenceFragment {
    @Override
    public void onCreate(Bundle savedInstanceState) {
        super.onCreate(savedInstanceState);
        addPreferencesFromResource(R.xml.sound_preferences);
    }
}
```

All this inner class needs to do is pull in the appropriate preferences XML file, as shown. That preferences XML file contains the types of preference specifications we covered earlier, such as ListPreference, CheckBoxPreference, PreferenceCategory, and so on. What's very nice is that Android takes care of doing the right thing when the screen configuration changes and when the preferences are displayed on a small screen. Headers behave like old preferences when the screen is too small to display both headers and the preference screen to the right. That is, you only see the headers; and when you click a header, you then see only the appropriate preference screen.

PreferenceScreens

The top-level container for preferences is a PreferenceScreen. Before tablets and PreferenceFragments, you could nest PreferenceScreens, and when the user clicked on a nested PreferenceScreen item, the new PreferenceScreen would replace the currently displayed PreferenceScreen. This worked fine on a small screen, but doesn't look as good on a tablet, especially if you started with headers and fragments. What you probably want is for the new PreferenceScreen to appear where the current fragment is.

To make a PreferenceScreen work inside of a fragment, all you need to do is specify a fragment class name for that PreferenceScreen. Listing 4-9 shows the XML from the sample application.

Listing 4-9. PreferenceScreen invoked via a PreferenceFragment

```
<PreferenceScreen
    android:title="Launch a new screen into a fragment"
    android:fragment="com.androidbook.preferences.main.BasicFrag" />
```

When the user clicks on this item, the current fragment is replaced with BasicFrag, which then loads a new XML layout for a PreferenceScreen as specified in nested_screen_basicfrag.xml. In this case, we chose not to make the BasicFrag class an inner class of the MainPreferenceActivity class, mainly because there is no sharing needed from the outer class, and to show you that you can do it this way if you prefer.

Dynamic Preference Summary Text

You've probably seen preferences where the preference summary contains the current value. This is actually a little harder to implement than you might think. To accomplish this feat, you create a listener callback that detects when a preference value is about to change, and you then update the preference summary accordingly. The first step is for your PreferenceFragment to implement the OnPreferenceChangeListener interface. You then need to implement the onPreferenceChange() callback. Listing 4-10 shows an example. The pkgPref object in the callback was set earlier to the preference in the onCreate() method.

Listing 4-10. Setting Up a Preference Listener

```
public boolean onPreferenceChange(Preference preference,
                                    Object newValue) {
    final String key = preference.getKey();
    if ("package_name_preference".equals(key)) {
        pkgPref.setSummary(newValue.toString());
    }
    ...
    return true;
}
```

You have to register the fragment as a listener in onResume() using setOnPre
ferenceChangeListener(this) on each preference you want to listen on, and
unregister in onPause() by calling it again with null. Now every time there is
a pending change to a preference you've registered for, this callback will be
invoked passing in the preference and the potential new value. The callback
returns a boolean indicating whether to proceed with setting the preference
to the new value (true) or not (false). Assuming you would return true to
allow the new setting, this is where you can update the summary value as
well. You could also validate the new value and reject the change. Perhaps
you want a MultiSelectListPreference to have a maximum number of
checked items. You could count the selected items in the callback and reject
the change if there are too many.

Saving State with Preferences

Preferences are great for allowing users to customize applications to their
liking, but we can use the Android preference framework for more than
that. When your application needs to keep track of some data between
invocations of the application, preferences are one way to accomplish the
task even if the user can't see the data in preference screens. Please find
the sample application called SavingStateDemo to follow along with the
complete source code.

The Activity class has a getPreferences(int mode) method. This, in
reality, simply calls getSharedPreferences() with the class name of the
activity as the tag plus the mode as passed in. The result is an activity-
specific shared preferences file that you can use to store data about this
activity across invocations. A simple example of how you could use this is
shown in Listing 4-11.

Listing 4-11. Using Preferences to Save State for an Activity

```
final String INITIALIZED = "initialized";
private String someString;
```

[...]

```
SharedPreferences myPrefs = getPreferences(MODE_PRIVATE);

boolean hasPreferences = myPrefs.getBoolean(INITIALIZED, false);
if(hasPreferences) {
    Log.v("Preferences", "We've been called before");
    // Read other values as desired from preferences file...
    someString = myPrefs.getString("someString", "");
}
else {
    Log.v("Preferences", "First time ever being called");
    // Set up initial values for what will end up
    // in the preferences file
    someString = "some default value";
}
```

[...]

```
// Later when ready to write out values
Editor editor = myPrefs.edit();
editor.putBoolean(INITIALIZED, true);
editor.putString("someString", someString);
// Write other values as desired
editor.commit();
```

What this code does is acquire a reference to preferences for our activity class and check for the existence of a boolean "preference" called `initialized`. We write "preference" in double quotation marks because this value is not something the user is going to see or set; it's merely a value that we want to store in a shared preferences file for use next time. If we get a value, the shared preferences file exists, so the application must have been called before. You could then read other values out of the shared preferences file. For example, someString could be an activity variable that should be set from the last time this activity ran or set to the default value if this is the first time.

To write values to the shared preferences file, you must first get a preferences `Editor`. You can then put values into preferences and commit those changes when you're finished. Note that, behind the scenes, Android is managing a `SharedPreferences` object that is truly shared. Ideally, there is never more than one `Editor` active at a time. But it is very important to call the commit() method so that the SharedPreferences object and the shared preferences XML file get updated. In the example, the value of someString is written out to be used the next time this activity runs.

You can access, write, and commit values any time to your preferences file. Possible uses for this include writing out high scores for a game or recording when the application was last run. You can also use the getSharedPreferences() call with different names to manage separate sets of preferences, all within the same application or even the same activity.

MODE_PRIVATE was used for mode in our examples thus far. Because the shared preferences files are always stored within your application's / data/data/{package} directory and therefore are not accessible to other applications, you only need to use MODE_PRIVATE.

Using DialogPreference

So far, you've seen how to use the out-of-the-box capabilities of the preferences framework, but what if you want to create a custom preference? What if you want something like the slider of the Brightness preference under Screen Settings? This is where DialogPreference comes in. DialogPreference is the parent class of EditTextPreference and ListPreference. The behavior is a dialog that pops up, displays choices to the user, and is closed with a button or via the Back button. But you can extend DialogPreference to set up your own custom preference. Within your extended class, you provide your own layout, your own click handlers, and custom code in onDialogClosed() to write the data for your preference to the shared preferences file.

Reference

Here are helpful references to topics you may wish to explore further:

- http://developer.android.com/design/patterns/ settings.html: Android's Design Guide to Settings. Some good advice about laying out Settings screens and options.

- http://developer.android.com/guide/topics/ui/ settings.html: Android's API Guide to Settings. This page describes the Settings framework.

- http://developer.android.com/reference/android/ provider/Settings.html: Reference page that lists the settings constants for calling a system settings activity.

- www.androidbook.com/androidfragments/projects:
  A list of downloadable projects related to this book. For
  this chapter, look for the file AndroidFragments_Ch04_
  Preferences.zip. This ZIP file contains all the projects
  from this chapter, listed in separate root directories.
  There is also a README.TXT file that describes how to
  import projects into your IDE from one of these ZIP files.

Summary

This chapter talked about managing preferences in Android:

- Types of preferences available

- Reading the current values of preferences into your
  application

- Setting default values from embedded code and by
  writing the default values from the XML file to the saved
  preferences file

- Organizing preferences into groups, and defining
  dependencies between preferences

- Callbacks on preferences to validate changes and to set
  dynamic summary text

- Using the preferences framework to save and restore
  information from an activity across invocations

- Creating a custom preference

Chapter 5

Using the Compatibility Library for Older Devices

The Android platform has gone through an impressive evolution since it was first introduced several years ago. While the intention has always been for Android to power lots of different types of devices, it wasn't architected from the beginning to meet that goal. Instead, the Google engineers have added, removed, and changed APIs in order to provide new features. One of the biggest changes was the creation of fragments in order to handle larger screen sizes such as on tablets and TVs. But there have been other changes such as with ActionBar and Menus.

The new APIs created a difficult problem for developers who wanted their applications to run on the new devices with the new APIs, as well as older devices that did not have those APIs. Many older devices do not get Android upgrades. Even if Google added the new APIs to a revision of the old Android OS, the old devices aren't going to get that new revision, because of the testing and support required from both the device manufacturer and the cellular carrier. The solution that Google came up with was to create compatibility libraries that could be linked into an application so it could take advantage of the new API functionality yet still run on an older version of Android. The library figures out how to use the older APIs to implement the new features. If the same application runs on a newer version of Android that already has those new features, the compatibility library calls through to the underlying APIs present in that newer version of Android.

This chapter will dive into the compatibility libraries and explain how to use them and what to watch out for. If you aren't developing applications for older versions of Android, you could safely skip this chapter as you won't need the libraries. The libraries are only useful if you want to include the functionality of a new API in an application that will run on an old version of Android that doesn't have that new API.

It All Started with Tablets

The Android operating system was doing fine until it came time to support tablets. The basic building block of an application was the activity, meant to perform a single task for the user and to fill the screen of the device. But tablets offered more real estate so the user could see and do a few things at a time on one screen. So with Honeycomb (Android 3.0), Google introduced fragments. This was a whole new concept, which changed how developers created UIs and the logic that ran behind them. And this would have been fine, except that there were still plenty of Android devices (e.g., smartphones) in the wild which did not support fragments. What Google figured out is that a compatibility library could be written to provide comparable implementations of Fragment, etc., that used the existing APIs in the older versions of Android. If an application linked in the compatibility library, it could work with fragments even though the older version of Android didn't support fragments in the OS.

The Google engineers then looked at other features and APIs in new Android and provided compatibility library features and APIs to match, so that these features could also be used in older versions of Android without having to release updates to those older versions of Android. In addition to support for Fragments, compatibility libraries provide support for Loaders, RenderScript, ActionBar, and others.

The compatibility library doesn't always make things perfectly the same between old and new. For example, the new Activity class is aware of fragments. To use the compatibility library, you must extend the FragmentActivity class instead of Activity; it is the FragmentActivity class that works with fragments in old Android versions.

When you use the compatibility library, you will use those classes for your application regardless of which version of Android it will run on. In other words, you would only use FragmentActivity in your application and it will do the right thing in all versions of Android, including Android 3.0 and later. You would not try to include in the same application both Activity for Android 3.0+ and FragmentActivity for Android below 3.0. When FragmentActivity is executing on Android 3.0 and above, it can pretty much call straight through to the underlying Activity class. There is no real penalty to using a compatibility library on a recent Android version.

Adding the Library to Your Project

As of this writing, there are four compatibility libraries; together the collection is called the Android Support Library, revision 21:

- v4—contains FragmentActivity, Fragment, Loader, and quite a few other classes introduced after Android 3.0. The number 4 represents Android API version 4 (i.e., Donut 1.6). It means this library can be used for applications that run on Android API version 4 and above.

- v7—makes available the ActionBar, CardView, GridLayout, MediaRouter, Palette and RecyclerView classes. This library can be used with Android API version 7 (i.e., Eclair 2.1) and above. There are actually six libraries here: appcompat, cardview, gridlayout, mediarouter, palette and recyclerview.

- v8—adds RenderScipt capability to Android API version 8 (i.e., Froyo 2.2) and above. RenderScript allows for parallelization of work across device processors (CPU cores, GPUs, DSPs) and was introduced in Android API version 11 (i.e., Honeycomb 3.0).

- v13—adds some special Fragment functionality for things like tabbed and pager interfaces. This library also contains many of the classes from v4 so it can be included in your application without requiring other libraries.

For a complete list of all compatibility functionality by version number, please see the references at the end of this chapter.

To download the Android Support Library to your computer, use the Android SDK Manager and look for it at the bottom of the list under Extras. If you're using Android Studio, download the Android Support Repository and Google Repository. Otherwise, download Android Support Library instead. The files will be placed under your Android SDK directory. The Android Support Library can be found in extras/android/support/, the Android Support Repository can be found in extras/android/m2repository, and the Google Repository can be found in extras/google/m2repository. As of this writing, the RenderScript compatibility library is not supported in Android Studio.

As you can see from the preceding bullet list, not all features of the Android Support Library are available on all older versions of Android. Therefore you must properly set android:minSdkVersion in your AndroidManifest.xml file. If you are using a compatibility library feature from v7, android:minSdkVersion should not be lower than 7.

Including the v7 Support Library

There's very little chance that you'd ever want to include the v4 library and not the v7 library. Since the v7 library requires that the v4 library also be included to provide the necessary classes for v7 to function properly, you'll want to include both. If you are using Eclipse, the ADT plug-in makes all of this pretty easy. When you create a new Android project in Eclipse, you specify the minimum version of Android that it will run on. If ADT thinks that you might want the compatibility library included, it will automatically include it.

For example, if you specify a target SDK of 16 (JellyBean 4.1) but a minimum SDK of 8 (Froyo 2.2), ADT will automatically set up an appcompat v7 library project, include that library project in your new application, and also include the v4 library as well in your application. The resources from the v7 library are therefore available to your application without you having to do extra work. However, if you want to use either of the other two v7 libraries (gridlayout and/or mediarouter), those will require a little extra work, as will now be explained. By creating a library project and including that in your application, it will include the compatibility library resources that your application will need.

You will manually do something similar to what ADT did to automatically include the v7 appcompat library into your project. To start, you will choose File ➤ Import, then Existing Android Code Into Workspace, then navigate to the extras folder where the Android SDK is on your workstation. Locate the v7 gridlayout or mediarouter folder and choose that. See Figure 5-1.

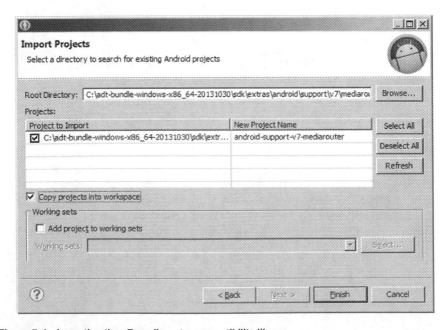

Figure 5-1. Importing the v7 mediarouter compatibility library

Click Finish and you will get a new library project. If you chose to create a library project for v7 mediarouter, you will see that it is missing some functionality so it has errors. You need to add in the v7 appcompat library to clear that up. Right-click the mediarouter library project in Eclipse and choose Properties. In the list on the left choose Android. Now click the Add... button in the Library section. See Figure 5-2.

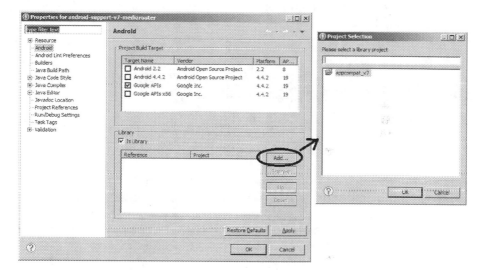

Figure 5-2. Adding appcompat_v7 to the v7 mediarouter compatibility library

Select the appcompat_v7 library and click OK. That should clear up the errors in mediarouter. Now when you want to include mediarouter in your application project, simply follow the same procedure but right-click your application project, and when you click the Add... button for Library, chose the mediarouter library.

Including the v8 Support Library

If you want to use the v8 renderscript compatibility library, you simply add the following two lines to the application project's project.properties file regardless of the target version of your application:

```
renderscript.target=19
renderscript.support.mode=true
```

If you see errors in the Eclipse Console regarding version numbers, try using a later version as indicated by the error. However, the very latest version of Android may not work for you either. The other thing you likely need to do is add the renderscript-v8.jar file as an external jar file to the project's Build Path. You will find this jar file under the SDK build-tools directory. Use the latest version available.

Within your code, make sure you import from android.support. v8.renderscript rather than android.renderscript. If you are modifying an existing RenderScript application for the v8 library, make sure to clean your project; the Java files that are generated from your .rs files need to be regenerated to also use the v8 library. You can now use RenderScript as usual and deploy your application to older versions of Android.

Including the v13 Support Library

Finally, to include the v13 compatibility library into your application, navigate to the SDK extras directory and find the v13 jar file. Copy this file to the / libs directory of your application project. Once the v13 jar file is in place, right-click it to pull up the menu, and then choose Build Path ➤ Add to Build Path. There's a good chance you already have the v4 and v7 appcompat libraries in your application courtesy of ADT. You may choose to get rid of those if you don't need the functionality from either one. For example, if the minimum SDK for your application is v11, you can use the native `ActionBar` class without the need for the v7 appcompat support library.

The v13 jar file contains many of the same classes as v4, so you don't want to cause any problems by having the same classes in twice. If you're going to have all three libraries in your application (i.e., v4, v7, and v13), then at least ensure that v13 is ordered before v4. This can be done in the Configure Build Path dialog box.

Including Just the v4 Support Library

If you really must have the v4 support library and none of the others, you would follow the same procedure as for the v13 library.

Retrofitting an App with the Android Support Library

To get a better feel for how this all works, you're going to bring back a fragment app you worked on in Chapter 1 and will make it work for older versions of Android that don't natively support fragments.

Use File ➤ Import, choose General, then Existing Projects into Workspace. Navigate to the ShakespeareInstrumented project from Chapter 1 and choose that. Check "Copy projects into workspace" before hitting Finish.

Now you're going to retrofit this application to work on versions of Android lower than API version 11. The following works when you don't need resources from the compatibility library, since it worries only about copying in the JAR file.

1. Right-click your project and choose Android Tools ➤ Add Support Library.... Accept the license and click OK.

2. Now go into `MainActivity.java` and change the base class from `Activity` to `FragmentActivity`. You need to fix the import line from `android.app.Activity` to `android.support.v4.app.FragmentActivity`. Also fix the imports for `Fragment`, `FragmentManager`, and `FragmentTransaction` to use the ones from the support library.

3. Find the method calls for `getFragmentManager()` and change these to `getSupportFragmentManager()`. Do this also for `DetailsActivity.java`.

4. For `DetailsFragment.java`, change the import for `Fragment` to the one for the support library `Fragment` (i.e., `android.support.v4.app.Fragment`).

5. In `TitlesFragment.java`, change the import for `ListFragment` to the one for the support library `ListFragment` (i.e., `android.support.v4.app.ListFragment`).

The newer versions of Android use different animators from old Android. You may need to fix animations in `MainActivity.java` in the `showDetails()` method. Pick one of the commented out calls to `setCustomAnimations()`, then play with the in and out animations. Anything that relies on an `ObjectAnimator` class will not work on older devices since this class was introduced with API version 11 (i.e., Honeycomb 3.0). It will compile but since that class has not been implemented in older Android and has not been included in the compatibility libraries, you will get a runtime exception. In other words, avoid R.animator. Try using R.anim instead. You can copy into your project anim resource files that you'd like to use, or you can try referring to `android.R.anim` files.

Now you can go into `AndroidManifest.xml` and change the `minSdkVersion` from 11 to 8. That should be all you need to do. Try running this application on a Froyo device or emulator. If all went well you should now be seeing a fragment-based application running on a pre–Android 3.0 OS.

References

Here are some helpful references to topics you may wish to explore further:

- `http://developer.android.com/tools/support-library/index.html`: The Android Developer's Guide on the Support Library package.

- `http://developer.android.com/tools/support-library/features.html`: Android documentation on the main features of each compatibility library.

- `http://developer.android.com/tools/support-library/setup.html`: Android documentation on setting up a compatibility library for your project, for both Eclipse and Android Studio. At the time of this writing, these pages were not as current as this chapter. However, things change. If you experience trouble, check the online documentation or contact the book's authors.

Summary

Let's conclude this chapter by quickly enumerating what you have learned about the Android compatibility libraries:

- To get your application working on the broadest array of devices, use the compatibility libraries and code to their APIs rather than the latest and greatest APIs.

- The v7 support libraries come with resources that must be included in your application for the APIs to work properly.

Chapter 6

Advanced AsyncTask and Progress Dialogs

In many Android applications, you will need to perform work behind the UI in a separate thread. While the work is going on, you might want to display some sort of progress indicator to the user. While it is possible to create your own threads, manage them, and coordinate UI updates from your thread, Android provides a couple of classes that take care of a lot of this for you automatically. Then you can focus on the actual work that you want to do, instead of the code for threads and messaging to the UI. The classes that do this are AsyncTask and ProgressDialog.

This chapter will start with the basics of an AsyncTask and move to the code needed to present progress dialogs and progress bars that show the status of an AsyncTask correctly even if the device changes its configuration.

Introducing the AsyncTask

Let's start by introducing the AsyncTask through pseudocode in Listing 6-1.

Listing 6-1. Usage Pattern for an AsyncTask by an Activity

```
public class MyActivity  {
    void respondToMenuItem()    { //menu handler
        performALongTask();
    }
}
```

```
void performALongTask()    { //using an AsyncTask
    //Derive from an AsyncTask, and Instantiate this AsyncTask
    MyLongTask myLongTask = new MyLongTask(...CallBackObjects...);
    myLongTask.execute(...someargs...); //start the work on a worker
    thread
    //have the main thread get back to its UI business
}

//Hear back from the AsyncTask
void someCallBackFromAsyncTask(SomeParameterizedType x)    {
    //Although invoked by the AsyncTask this code runs on the main
    thread.
    //report back to the user of the progress
}
}
```

Use of an AsyncTask starts with extending from AsyncTask first like the MyLongTask in Listing 6-1. Once you have the AsyncTask object instantiated, you can call execute() method on that object. The execute() method internally starts a separate thread to do the actual work. The AsyncTask implementation will in turn invoke a number of callbacks to report the beginning of the task, the progress of the task, and the end of the task. Listing 6-2 shows pseudocode to extend an AsyncTask and the methods that need to be overridden. (Please note that this is pseudocode and not intended to be compiled. The @Override annotation is added to explicitly state that they are overridden from the base class).

Listing 6-2. Extending an AsyncTask: An Example

```
public class MyLongTask extends AsyncTask<String,Integer,Integer> {
    //... constructors stuff
    //Calling execute() will result in calling all of these methods
    @Override
    void onPreExecute(){} //Runs on the main thread

    //This is where you do all the work and runs on the worker thread
    @Override
    Integer doInBackground(String... params){}

    //Runs on the main thread again once it finishes
    @Override
    void onPostExecute(Integer result){}

    //Runs on the main thread
    @Override
    void onProgressUpdate(Integer... progressValuesArray){}
    //....other methods
}
```

execute( ) method in Listing 6-1 is called on the main thread. This call will trigger a series of methods in Listing 6-2, starting with onPreExecute(). The onPreExecute() is called on the main thread as well. You can use this method to set up your environment to execute the task. You can also use this method to set up a dialog box or initiate a progress bar to indicate to the user that the work has started. After the completion of the onPreExecute(), execute() method will return and the main thread of the activity continues with its UI responsibilities. By that time the execute() would have spawned a new worker thread so that doInBackground() method is scheduled to be executed on that worker thread. You will do all your heavy lifting in this doInBackground() method. As this method runs on a worker thread, the main thread is not affected and you will not get the "application not responding" message. From the doInBackground() method you have a facility (you will see this shortly) to call the onProgressUpdate() to report the progress. This onProgressUpdate() method runs on the main thread so that you can affect the UI on the main thread.

Implementing a Simple AsyncTask

Let's get into the details of extending the AsyncTask. The AsyncTask class uses generics to provide type safety to its methods, including the overridden methods. You can see these generics when you look at the partial definition (Listing 6-3) of the AsyncTask class. (Please note that Listing 6-3 is an extremely pruned-down version of the AsyncTask class. It's really just the elements of its interface most commonly used by client code.)

Listing 6-3. A Quick Look at the AsyncTask Class Definition

```
public class AsyncTask<Params, Progress, Result> {
    //A client will call this method
    AsyncTask<Params, Progress, Result>    execute(Params... params);

    //Do your work here. Frequently triggers onProgressUpdate( )
    Result doInBackground(Params... params);

    //Callback: After the work is complete
    void onPostExecute(Result result);

    //Callback: As the work is progressing
    void onProgressUpdate(Progress... progressValuesArray);
}
```

Studying Listing 6-3, you can see that the AsyncTask (through generics) needs the following three parameterized types (Params, Progress, and Result) when you extend it. Let's explain these types briefly:

- ▓   Params (The type of parameters to the execute( ) method): When extending AsyncTask, you will need to indicate the type of parameters that you will pass to the execute( ) method. If you say your Params type is String, then the execute( ) method will expect any number of strings separated by commas in its invocation such as execute(s1,s2,s3) or execute(s1,s2,s3,s4,s5).

- ▓   Progress (Parameter types to the progress callback method): This type indicates the array of values passed back to the caller while reporting progress through the callback onProgressUpdate(Progress... progressValuesArray). The ability to pass an array of progress values allows situations where multiple aspects of a task can be monitored and reported on. For example, this feature could be used if an AsyncTask is working on multiple subtasks.

- ▓   Result (Type used to report the result through onPostExecute( ) method): This type indicates the type of the data returned by doInBackground(), which is ultimately passed to onPostExecute() for handling in a thread-safe manner.

Knowing now the needed generic types for an AsyncTask, suppose we decide on the following parameters for our specific AsyncTask: Params: A String, Result: An Integer, Progress: An Integer. Then, we can declare an extended AsyncTask class as shown in Listing 6-4.

Listing 6-4. Extending the Generic AsyncTask Through Concrete Types

```
public class MyLongTask
extends AsyncTask<String,Integer,Integer>
{
    //...other constructors stuff
    //...other methods
    //Concrete methods based on the parameterized types
    protected Integer doInBackground(String... params){}
    protected void onPostExecute(Integer result){}
    protected void onProgressUpdate(Integer... progressValuesArray){}

    //....other methods
}
```

Notice how this concrete class in Listing 6-4, MyLongTask, has disambiguated the type names and arrived at function signatures that are type safe.

Implementing Your First AsyncTask

Let's now look at a simple, but complete, implementation of MyLongTask. We have amply commented the code in Listing 6-5 inline to indicate which methods run on which thread. Also pay attention to the constructor of MyLongTask where it receives object references of the calling context (usually an activity) and also a specific simple interface such as IReportBack to log progress messages.

The IReportBack interface is not critical to your understanding because it is merely a wrapper to a log. Same is true with the Utils class as well. You can see these additional classes in both of the downloadable projects for this chapter. The URL for the downloadable projects is in the references section at the end of this chapter. Listing 6-5 shows the complete code for MyLongTask.

Listing 6-5. Complete Source Code for Implementing an AsyncTask

```
//The following code is in MyLongTask.java (AndroidFragments_Ch06_
TestAsyncTask.zip)
//Use menu item: Test Async1 to invoke this code
public class MyLongTask extends AsyncTask<String,Integer,Integer>
{
    IReportBack r; // an interface to report back log messages
    Context ctx;      //The activity to start a dialog
    public String tag = null;  //Debug tag
    ProgressDialog pd = null;  //To start, report, and stop a progress
    dialog

    //Constructor now
    MyLongTask(IReportBack inr, Context inCtx, String inTag)   {
        r = inr;  ctx = inCtx;  tag = inTag;
    }
    //Runs on the main ui thread
    protected void onPreExecute()     {
        Utils.logThreadSignature(this.tag);
        pd = ProgressDialog.show(ctx, "title", "In Progress...",true);
    }
```

```
//Runs on the main ui thread. Triggered by publishProgress called
multiple times
protected void onProgressUpdate(Integer... progress)  {
    Utils.logThreadSignature(this.tag);
    Integer i = progress[0];
    r.reportBack(tag, "Progress:" + i.toString());
}
protected void onPostExecute(Integer result)      {
    //Runs on the main ui thread
    Utils.logThreadSignature(this.tag);
    r.reportBack(tag, "onPostExecute result:" + result);
    pd.cancel();
}
//Runs on a worker thread. May even be a pool if there are more tasks.
protected Integer doInBackground(String...strings)    {
    Utils.logThreadSignature(this.tag);
    for(String s :strings)         {
        Log.d(tag, "Processing:" + s);
    }
    for (int i=0;i<3;i++)          {
        Utils.sleepForInSecs(2);
        publishProgress(i); //this calls onProgressUpdate
    }
    return 1; //this value is then passed to the onPostExecute as input
    }
}
```

We will go into the details of each of the methods highlighted in Listing 6-5 after covering briefly how a client would make use of (or call) MyLongTask.

Calling an AsyncTask

Once we have the class MyLongTask implemented, a client will utilize this class as shown in Listing 6-6.

Listing 6-6. Calling an AsyncTask

```
//You will find this class AsyncTester.java(AndroidFragments_Ch06_
TestAsyncTask.zip)
//Use menu item: Test Async1 to invoke this code
void respondToMenuItem() {
    //An interface to log some messages back to the activity
    //See downloadable project if you need the details.
    IReportBack reportBackObject = this;
    Context ctx = this; //activity
    String tag = "Task1"; //debug tag
```

```
    //Instantiate and execute the long task
    MyLongTask mlt = new MyLongTask(reportBackObject,ctx,tag);
    mlt.execute("String1","String2","String3");
}
```

Notice how the execute( ) method is called in Listing 6-6. Because we have indicated one of the generic types as a String and that the execute( ) method takes a variable number of arguments for this type, we can pass any number of strings to the execute( ) method. In the example in Listing 6-6, we have passed three string arguments. You can pass more or less as you need.

Once we call the execute( ) method on the AsyncTask, this will result in a call to the onPreExecute( ) method followed by a call to the doInBackground( ) method. The system will also call the onPostExecute( ) callback once the doInBackground( ) method finishes. Refer to Listing 6-5 for how these methods are implemented.

Understanding the onPreExecute( ) Callback and Progress Dialog

Going back to MyLongTask implementation in Listing 6-5, in the onPreExecute( ) method we started a progress dialog to indicate that the task is in progress. Figure 6-1 shows an image of that dialog. (Use menu item Test Async1 to invoke this view from project download AndroidFragments_Ch06_TestAsyncTask.zip.)

Figure 6-1. A simple progress dialog interacting with an AsyncTask

The code segment (taken from Listing 6-5) that shows the progress dialog is reproduced in Listing 6-7.

Listing 6-7. Showing an Indeterminate Progress Dialog

```
pd = ProgressDialog.show(ctx, "title", "In Progress...",true);
```

The variable pd was already declared in the constructor (see Listing 6-5). This call in Listing 6-7 will create a progress dialog and display it as shown in Figure 6-1. The last argument to the show( ) method in Listing 6-7 indicates if the dialog is indeterminate (whether the dialog can estimate beforehand how much work there is). We will cover the deterministic case in a later section.

> **Note**   Showing progress of an AsyncTask reliably is quite involved. This is because an activity can come and go, because of either a configuration change or another UI taking precedence. We will cover this essential need and solution later in the chapter.

Understanding the doInBackground( ) Method

All the background work carried out by the AsyncTask is done in the doInBackground( ) method. This method is orchestrated by the AsyncTask to run on a worker thread. As a result, this work is allowed to take more than five seconds, unlike the work done on a main thread.

In our example from Listing 6-5, in the doInBackground( ) method we simply retrieve each of the input strings to the task as if they are an array. In this method definition we haven't defined an explicit string array. However, the single argument to this function is defined as a variable-length argument, as shown in Listing 6-8.

Listing 6-8. doInBackground( ) Method Signature

```
protected Integer doInBackground(String...strings)
```

Java then treats the argument as if it is an array inside the function. So in our code in the doInBackground( ) method, we read each of the strings and log them to indicate that we know what they are. We then wait long enough to simulate a long-running operation. Because this method is running in a worker thread, we should not access the UI functionality of Android from this worker thread. For instance, you should not update any Views directly even if you have access to them from this thread. You cannot even send a Toast from here. The next two methods allow us to overcome this.

Triggering onProgressUpdate() through publishProgress()

In the doInBackground() method, you can trigger onProgressUpdate() by calling the publishProgress() method. The triggered onProgressUpdate() method then runs on the main thread. This allows the onProgressUpdate() method to update UI elements such as Views appropriately. You can also send a Toast from here. In Listing 6-5, we simply log a message. Once all the work is done, we return from the doInBackground() method with a result code.

Understanding the onPostExecute() Method

The result code from the doInBackground() method is then passed to the onPostExecute() callback method. This callback is also executed on the main thread. In this method, we tell the progress dialog to close. Being on the main thread, you can access any UI elements in this method with no restrictions.

Upgrading to a Deterministic Progress Dialog

In the previous example in Listing 6-5, we used a progress dialog (Figure 6-1) that doesn't tell us what portion of the work is complete. This progress dialog is called an indeterminate progress dialog. If you set the indeterminate property to false on this progress dialog, you will see a progress dialog that tracks progress in steps. This is shown in Figure 6-2. (Use menu item "Test Async 2" to invoke this view from project download AndroidFragments_Ch06_TestAsyncTask.zip.)

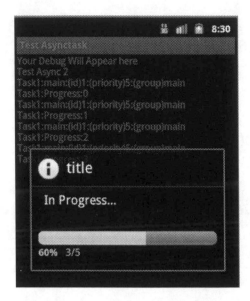

Figure 6-2. A progress dialog showing explicit progress, interacting with an AsyncTask

Listing 6-9 shows the previous task from Listing 6-5 rewritten to change the behavior of the progress dialog to a deterministic progress dialog. We have also added an onCancelListener to see if we need to cancel the task on cancelling the dialog. A user can click the back button in Figure 6-2 to cancel the dialog. Key portions of the code are given in Listing 6-9 (for the full code, see the download file AndroidFragments_Ch06_TestAsyncTask.zip).

Listing 6-9. A Long Task Utilizing a Deterministic Progress Dialog

```
//Following code is in MyLongTask1.java(AndroidFragments_Ch06_TestAsyncTask.zip)
//Use menu item: Test Async2 to invoke this code
public class MyLongTask1 extends AsyncTask<String,Integer,Integer>
implements OnCancelListener
{
    //..other code taken from Listing 6-5
    //Also refer to the java class MyLongTask1.java in the downloadable project
    //for full code listing.
    protected void onPreExecute()    {
        //....other code
        pd = new ProgressDialog(ctx);
        pd.setTitle("title");
        pd.setMessage("In Progress...");
        pd.setCancelable(true);
        pd.setOnCancelListener(this);
        pd.setIndeterminate(false);
```

```
        pd.setProgressStyle(ProgressDialog.STYLE_HORIZONTAL);
        pd.setMax(5);
        pd.show();
    }
    public void onCancel(DialogInterface d)    {
        r.reportBack(tag,"Cancel called on the dialog");
        this.cancel(true);
    }
    //..other code taken from Listing 6-5
}
```

Notice how we have prepared the progress dialog in Listing 6-9. In this case we haven't used the static method show( ), in contrast to what we did in Listing 6-5, on the progress dialog. Instead, we explicitly instantiated the progress dialog. The variable ctx stands for the context (or activity) in which this UI progress dialog operates. Then we individually set the properties on the dialog, including its deterministic or indeterminate behavior. The method setMax( ) indicates how many steps the progress dialog has. We have also passed the self reference (the AsyncTask itself) as a listener when a dialog cancel is triggered. In the cancel callback, we explicitly issue a cancel on the AsyncTask. The cancel( ) method with a boolean argument of false will set a flag on the AsyncTask which can be queried with isCancelled(). The doInBackground() method should periodically check isCancelled() to gracefully end early if cancelled. A boolean argument of true will force-stop the worker thread.

AsyncTask and Thread Pools

Consider the code in Listing 6-10, where a menu item is invoking two AsyncTasks one after the other.

Listing 6-10. Invoking Two Long-Running Tasks

```
void respondToMenuItem( ) {
    MyLongTask mlt = new MyLongTask(this.mReportTo,this.mContext,"Task1");
    mlt.execute("String1","String2","String3");

    MyLongTask mlt1 = new MyLongTask(this.mReportTo,this.mContext,"Task2");
    mlt1.execute("String1","String2","String3");
}
```

Here we are executing two tasks on the main thread. You may expect that both the tasks get started close to each other. The default behavior, however, is that these tasks run sequentially using a single thread drawn out of a pool of threads. If you want a parallel execution, you can use the executeOnExecutor() method on the AsyncTask. See the reference documentation of AsyncTask for details on this method. Also as per the SDK documentation, it is not valid to call the execute() method more than once on a single AsyncTask. If you want that behavior, you have to instantiate a new task and call the execute() method again.

Issues and Solutions for Correctly Showing the Progress of an AsyncTask

If your primary goal with this chapter is to learn just the essentials of AsyncTask, then what we have covered so far is sufficient. However, there are some issues when an AsyncTask is paired with a progress dialog as shown in the previous listings so far. One of those issues is that an AsyncTask will lose the correct activity reference when the device is rotated, thereby also losing its reference to the progress dialog. The other issue is that the progress dialog we used earlier in the code is not a managed dialog. Let's understand these issues now.

Dealing with Activity Pointers and Device Rotation

The activity pointer that is held by the AsyncTask becomes stale when the activity is re-created because of a configuration change. This is because Android has created a new activity and the old activity is no longer shown on the screen. So holding on to the old activity and its corresponding dialog is bad for a couple of reasons. The first is that the user is not seeing that activity or dialog that the AsyncTask is trying to update. The second reason is that the old activity needs to be garbage collected and you are stopping it from getting garbage collected because the AsyncTask is holding on to its reference. If you were to be smart and use a Java weak reference for the old activity, then you wouldn't leak memory but you would get a null pointer exception. The case of a stale pointer is true not only of the activity pointer but any other pointer that indirectly points to the activity.

The recommended way to address the stale activity reference issue is to use headless retained fragments. (Fragments are covered in Chapter 1. Retained fragments are fragments that stay around while the activity is re-created due to a configuration change. These fragments are also called headless because they don't necessarily have to hold any UI.)

Dealing with Managed Dialogs

Even if we are able to solve the stale activity reference issue and reestablish the connectivity to the current activity, there is a flaw in the way progress dialogs were used so far in this chapter. We have instantiated a ProgressDialog directly. A ProgressDialog created in this manner is not a "managed" dialog. If it is not a managed dialog, the activity will not re-create the dialog when the device undergoes rotation or any other configuration change. So, when the device rotates the AsyncTask is still running uninterrupted but the dialog will not show up. There are a couple of ways to solve this problem as well. The recommended way is not to use progress dialogs but instead use an embedded UI control in the activity itself, such as a progress bar. Because a progress bar is part of the activity view hierarchy, the hope is that it will be re-created. Although a progress bar sounds good, there are times when a modal progress dialog makes more sense. For example, that would be the case if you don't want the user to interact with any other part of the activity while the AsyncTask is running. In those cases, we see little contradiction in using fragment dialogs instead of progress bars.

The solution you will see next uses a retained non-UI fragment plus a progress dialog that is recreated as necessary if and when the activity is recreated due to a configuration change. There are other ways that you might choose to implement a progress indicator, and they could use a similar technique.

Testing Scenarios for a Well-Behaved Progress Dialog

Whichever solution you use to correctly display a progress dialog for an AsyncTask, the solution should work in all of the following test scenarios:

1. Without an orientation change the progress dialog must start, show its progress, end, and also clean up the reference to the AsyncTask. This must work repeatedly to show that there are no vestiges left from the previous run.

2. The solution should handle the orientation changes while the task is in the middle of its execution. The rotation should re-create the dialog and show progress where it left off. The dialog should properly finish and clean up the AsyncTask reference. This must work repeatedly to show that there are no vestiges left behind.

3.   Going Home should be allowed even when the task is in the middle of execution.

4.   Going Home and revisiting the activity should show the dialog and correctly reflect the current progress, and the progress should never be less than the one before.

5.   Going Home and revisiting the activity also should work when the task finishes before returning. The dialog should be properly dismissed and the AsyncTask reference removed.

This set of test cases should always be performed for all activities dealing with AsyncTasks. Now that we have laid out how a solution should satisfy, let's show one that uses a retained fragment and progress dialog.

Using a Retained Fragment and a Progress Dialog

In this solution, let's show you how to use a retained fragment and a progress dialog for displaying progress correctly for an AsyncTask. This solution involves the following steps:

1.   The activity must keep track of non-UI fragment. This external fragment must stick around and its reference validated as the activity is closed and brought back. This retained fragment holds a reference to the AsyncTask.

2.   A retained fragment then will have a pointer to the AsyncTask and can set and reset the activity pointer on AsyncTask as the activity comes and goes. So, this retained fragment acts as an intermediary between the activity and the AsyncTask.

3.   The AsyncTask then will instantiate a progress dialog. The AsyncTask will use the activity pointer that is set by the retained fragment to accomplish this, as you will need an activity to create a progress dialog.

4.   The AsyncTask will re-create the dialog as the device rotates and keeps its state properly.

5. A user can go Home by tapping Home and use other apps. This will push our activity, and the dialog with it, into the background. This must be handled. When the user returns to the activity or app, the dialog can continue to show the progress. The AsyncTask must know how to dismiss the dialog if the task finishes while the activity is hidden.

Exploring Key Code Snippets

We will present now the key pieces of code that are used to implement the outlined approach. The rest of the implementation can be found in the downloadable project AndroidFragments_Ch06_TestAsyncTask2.zip for this chapter. Listing 6-11 presents the source code of the retained fragment first. This fragment manages the AsyncTask on behalf of the activity.

Listing 6-11. Managing an AsyncTask with a Retained non-UI Fragment

```
public class AsyncTaskFragment extends Fragment {
    private static final String tag = "AsyncTaskFragment";
    private TestAsyncTaskDriverActivity ctx = null;
    private MyLongTask mlt = null;

    public static AsyncTaskFragment newInstance(String... params) {
        AsyncTaskFragment myMF = new AsyncTaskFragment();
        Bundle bundle = new Bundle();
        bundle.putStringArray("params", params);
        myMF.setArguments(bundle);
        return myMF;
    }

    @Override
    public void onAttach(Activity activity) {
        super.onAttach(activity);
        ctx = (TestAsyncTaskDriverActivity) activity;
        if(mlt != null &&
            mlt.getStatus() != AsyncTask.Status.FINISHED) {
            // we must have an incomplete task, make
            // sure it has the correct activity
            mlt.setActivity(activity);
        }
```

```
        else {
            mlt = new MyLongTask(ctx, ctx, "Task1");
            String[] params = this.getArguments()
                            .getStringArray("params");
            mlt.execute(params);
        }
    }

    @Override
    public void onCreate(Bundle savedInstanceState) {
        super.onCreate(savedInstanceState);
        setRetainInstance(true);
    }

    // When the activity is going away, make sure
    // to dismiss the dialog if it's there.
    @Override
    public void onDetach() {
        super.onDetach();
        Log.d(tag, "calling for dismissal of the dialog");
        if(mlt != null) {
            mlt.dismissDialog();
        }
    }
}
```

Code in Listing 6-11 shows how to set up a non-UI fragment as a go-between from the activity to the AsyncTask. By setting the fragment to be retained, it will survive configuration changes. It also takes the list of strings from the activity and easily passes those on to the AsyncTask. However, the AsyncTask is going to invoke UI changes on the activity and not on this fragment. Since the fragment will get notified when the activity is going away (i.e., via the onDetach() callback), it can let the AsyncTask know to dismiss the dialog. The fragment also knows when the activity gets attached to this fragment, and if there is an already-running AsyncTask. It means the activity has been recreated due to a configuration change. Therefore, this fragment can notify the AsyncTask of the new activity so it can re-generate the progress dialog. If there is not a running AsyncTask, this fragment creates a new one and executes it.

Let's see now how an AsyncTask can create and control this progress dialog. Listing 6-12 presents the code for the AsyncTask in order to aid this understanding.

Listing 6-12. AsyncTask That Uses a Progress Dialog

```java
public class MyLongTask
extends AsyncTask<String,Integer,Integer>
implements OnCancelListener
{
    private IReportBack r;
    private Context ctx;
    private String tag = null;
    private ProgressDialog pd = null;
    final private int PDMAX = 5;
    private int pd_progress = 0;
    MyLongTask(IReportBack inr, Context inCtx, String inTag)
    {
        r = inr;
        ctx = inCtx;
        tag = inTag;
    }
    protected void onPreExecute()
    {
        //Runs on the main ui thread
        Utils.logThreadSignature(this.tag);
        pd = newPDinstance(0);
        pd.show();
    }
    protected void onProgressUpdate(Integer... progress)
    {
        //Runs on the main ui thread
        Utils.logThreadSignature(this.tag);
        this.reportThreadSignature();

        //will be called multiple times
        //triggered by onPostExecute
        Integer i = progress[0];
        r.reportBack(tag, "Progress:" + i.toString());
        pd.setProgress(i);
    }
    protected void onPostExecute(Integer result)
    {
        //Runs on the main ui thread
        Utils.logThreadSignature(this.tag);
        r.reportBack(tag, "onPostExecute result:" + result);
        pd.cancel();
        r.allDone(0);
    }
```

```java
protected Integer doInBackground(String...strings)
{
    //Runs on a worker thread
    //May even be a pool if there are
    //more tasks.
    Utils.logThreadSignature(this.tag);

    for(String s :strings)
    {
        Log.d(tag, "Processing:" + s);
    }
    for (int i=0;i<PDMAX;i++)
    {
        Utils.sleepForInSecs(2);
        publishProgress(i+1);
        if(isCancelled()) {
            Log.e(tag, "*** This task has been cancelled");
            break;
        }
    }
    return 1;
}

public void onCancelled(Integer result) {
    Log.d(tag, "AsyncTask was cancelled");
    r.allDone(1);
}

protected void reportThreadSignature()
{
    String s = Utils.getThreadSignature();
    r.reportBack(tag,s);
}

public void onCancel(DialogInterface d)
{
    r.reportBack(tag,"Cancel called on the dialog");
    // Therefore, cancel the AsyncTask
    this.cancel(false);
}

// Must detach the progress dialog from the
// activity before it's gone away, otherwise
// we'll get a window leaked exception.
public void dismissDialog() {
    if(pd != null) {
        pd_progress = pd.getProgress();
        pd.dismiss();
    }
}
```

```
    // When there's a new activity, need to kill the
    // old dialog and create a new one, but with the
    // latest progress.
    public void setActivity(Context newCtx) {
        r = (IReportBack)newCtx;
        ctx = newCtx;
        pd = newPDinstance(pd_progress);
        pd.show();
    }

    private ProgressDialog newPDinstance(int progress) {
        ProgressDialog newPD = new ProgressDialog(ctx);
        newPD.setTitle("title");
        newPD.setMessage("In progress...");
        newPD.setCancelable(true);
        newPD.setOnCancelListener(this);
        newPD.setIndeterminate(false);
        newPD.setProgressStyle(ProgressDialog.STYLE_HORIZONTAL);
        newPD.setMax(PDMAX);
        newPD.setProgress(progress);
        return newPD;
    }
}
```

This AsyncTask in Listing 6-12 looks a lot like the earlier one from the beginning of this chapter. It handles the management of its progress dialog so that it acts like a cohesive unit and thereby doesn't contaminate the main activity with the details of this AsyncTask. It does, however, use a new method in the IReportBack interface, to allow this AsyncTask to tell the activity when it is finished. You will see in Listing 6-13 that the activity uses the allDone() method to get rid of the retained fragment that managed this AsyncTask. This is how the cleanup is done. You should notice that the progress dialog gets instantiated in two different places: in the onPreExecute() callback when the AsyncTask is starting up for the first time, and in setActivity() when there's a new activity and therefore a new dialog is required.

When creating the progress dialog in setActivity(), the last known progress value is used to start the dialog where it left off. To ensure no memory leaks, the dismissDialog() method is provided to the retained fragment so the dialog can be removed before the activity is destroyed. The retained fragment knows the activity is going away because of its onDetach() callback.

Listing 6-13 shows the activity that calls the retained fragment to setup the AsyncTask. You should notice that there are no references to an AsyncTask within the activity code, only the fragment is known to the activity.

Listing 6-13. Activity that calls the Retained Fragment

```java
public class TestAsyncTaskDriverActivity extends Activity
implements IReportBack
{
    public static final String tag="TestAsyncTaskDriverActivity";
    private static final String ASYNCTASKFRAG = "ASYNCTASKFRAG";

    private AsyncTaskFragment atf = null;
    @Override
    public void onCreate(Bundle savedInstanceState) {
        super.onCreate(savedInstanceState);
        setContentView(R.layout.main);
        if ((atf = (AsyncTaskFragment) getFragmentManager()
                .findFragmentByTag(ASYNCTASKFRAG)) != null) {
            // we found an incomplete AsyncTask in the background
            Log.d(tag, "Found an incomplete AsyncTask");
        }
    }

    @Override
    public boolean onCreateOptionsMenu(Menu menu){
        super.onCreateOptionsMenu(menu);
            MenuInflater inflater = getMenuInflater();
            inflater.inflate(R.menu.main_menu, menu);
        return true;
    }
    @Override
    public boolean onOptionsItemSelected(MenuItem item){
        appendMenuItemText(item);
        if (item.getItemId() == R.id.menu_clear){
            this.emptyText();
            return true;
        }
        if (item.getItemId() == R.id.menu_test_async1){
            if(atf == null) {
                atf = AsyncTaskFragment
                    .newInstance("String1","String2","String3");
                getFragmentManager().beginTransaction()
                    .add(atf, ASYNCTASKFRAG).commit();
            }
            return true;
        }
        return true;
    }
    private TextView getTextView(){
        return (TextView)this.findViewById(R.id.text1);
    }
```

```
    private void appendMenuItemText(MenuItem menuItem){
        String title = menuItem.getTitle().toString();
        TextView tv = getTextView();
        tv.setText(tv.getText() + "\n" + title);
    }
    private void emptyText(){
        TextView tv = getTextView();
        tv.setText("");
    }
    private void appendText(String s){
        TextView tv = getTextView();
        tv.setText(tv.getText() + "\n" + s);
        Log.d(tag,s);
    }
    public void reportBack(String tag, String message)
    {
        this.appendText(tag + ":" + message);
        Log.d(tag,message);
    }
    public void reportTransient(String tag, String message)
    {
        String s = tag + ":" + message;
        Toast.makeText(this, s, Toast.LENGTH_SHORT).show();
        reportBack(tag,message);
        Log.d(tag,message);
    }

    public void allDone(int status) {
        // Could do various things based on the returned status
        // but need to throw away the fragment so we can do this
        // again if needed.
        Log.d(tag, "AsyncTask returned: " + status);
        getFragmentManager().beginTransaction()
            .remove(atf).commitAllowingStateLoss();
        atf = null;
    }
}
```

There are really just three places that the activity deals with the fragment. In the onCreate() callback, the activity checks to see if there is an existing retained fragment and if it exists, Android will automatically re-attach It to the activity.

The menu click code will create a new retained fragment (and therefore the associated AsyncTask) if one is not already there. We do not want more than one at a time. And finally, in the allDone() callback, the retained fragment will be destroyed when it is finished performing its duties. Notice the commitAllowingStateLoss() method in allDone(). This is used because the activity may not be visible, but we still want to attempt to remove the retained fragment. If regular commit() is used, an exception will be thrown.

There are further considerations if the AsyncTask were doing updates and changing state. If that is the case, you may want to use a background service so that it can be restarted if the process is to be reclaimed and restarted later. You could also consider using a notification to track progress of some background task related to your application, similar to how the Google Play Store shows you the progress of applications that are being downloaded and installed/upgraded. The approaches presented here are adequate for quick- to medium-level reads as you are expecting the user to wait. However, for longer-time reads or writes, you may want to adapt a service-based solution.

References

The following references will help you learn more about the topics discussed in this chapter:

- http://developer.android.com/reference/android/os/AsyncTask.html: A key resource that definitively documents the behavior of AsyncTask.

- www.shanekirk.com/2012/04/asynctask-missteps/: Another look at a well-behaved AsyncTask.

- www.androidbook.com/item/3536: Research notes on AsyncTask that we gathered in preparing this chapter.

- www.androidbook.com/item/3537: Android uses Java generics often in its API. This URL documents a few basics on Java generics to get you started.

- www.androidbook.com/fragments: As this chapter has demonstrated, to work with an AsyncTask authoritatively you need to know a lot about activity life cycle, fragments, their life cycle, headless fragments, configuration changes, fragment dialogs, AsyncTask, and more. This URL has a number of articles focusing on all these areas.

- www.androidbook.com/item/4660: ADO is an abstraction that one of our authors espoused as a handy tool to deal with configuration change. This URL documents what ADOs are and how they could be used, and it also provides a preliminary implementation.

- www.androidbook.com/item/4674: This URL documents the background, helpful URLs, code snippets, and helpful hints to work with a ProgressBar.

- www.androidbook.com/item/4680: This URL has a good bit of research on activity life cycle in the event of configuration changes.

- www.androidbook.com/item/4665: It is quite hard to write programs that work well when devices rotate. This URL outlines some basic test cases you must successfully run for validating AsyncTask.

- www.androidbook.com/item/4673: This URL suggests an enhanced pattern for constructing inherited fragments.

- www.androidbook.com/item/4629: The best way to understand a fragment, including a retained fragment, is to study its callbacks diligently. This URL provides documented sample code for all the important callbacks of a fragment.

- www.androidbook.com/item/4668: The best way to understand an activity life cycle is study its callbacks diligently. This URL provides documented sample code for all the important activity callbacks.

- www.androidbook.com/item/3634: This URL outlines our research on fragment dialogs.

- www.androidbook.com/AndroidFragments/projects: A list of downloadable projects from this book is at this URL. For this chapter, look for a zip file named AndroidFragments_Ch06_AsyncTask.zip.

Summary

In this chapter, in addition to covering AsyncTask, we have introduced you to progress dialogs, and headless retained fragments. Reading this chapter, you not only understood AsyncTask but also got to apply your understanding of activity life cycle and a deep understanding of fragments. We have also documented a set of key test cases that must be satisfied for a well-behaved Android application.

Index

S

T, U

V, W, X, Y

Z

Get the eBook for only $10!

Now you can take the weightless companion with you anywhere, anytime. Your purchase of this book entitles you to 3 electronic versions for only $10.

This Apress title will prove so indispensible that you'll want to carry it with you everywhere, which is why we are offering the eBook in 3 formats for only $10 if you have already purchased the print book.

Convenient and fully searchable, the PDF version enables you to easily find and copy code—or perform examples by quickly toggling between instructions and applications. The MOBI format is ideal for your Kindle, while the ePUB can be utilized on a variety of mobile devices.

Go to www.apress.com/promo/tendollars to purchase your companion eBook.